Successful Retailing through Advertising

Successful Retailing through Advertising

Eric Lowe

McGRAW-HILL Book Company (UK) Limited

London · New York · St Louis · San Francisco · Auckland
Bogotá · Guatemala · Hamburg · Johannesburg · Lisbon
Madrid · Mexico · Montreal · New Delhi · Panama · Paris
San Juan · Saõ Paulo · Singapore · Sydney · Tokyo · Toronto

Published by
McGRAW-HILL Book Company (UK) Limited
MAIDENHEAD · BERKSHIRE · ENGLAND

British Library Cataloguing in Publication Data
Lowe, Eric.
  Successful retailing through advertising.
  1. Advertising.
  I. Title.
  659.1   HF5821
ISBN 0–07–084588–3

Library of Congress Cataloging in Publication Data
Lowe, Eric.
  Successful retailing through advertising.
  Includes index.
  1. Advertising.   I. Title.
HF5821.L675   1983   659.1   82–22952
ISBN 0–07–084588–3

1 2 3 4 5 MoC 8 6 5 4 3

Typeset by Phoenix Photosetting, Chatham
Printed and bound in Great Britain by
Mackays of Chatham Ltd

Contents

Preface

This book is intended for the small independent retailers who, despite intense competitive pressure from large chain stores, manage their shops and still retain approximately 40 per cent of all retail sales.

I have mingled with these retailers for 30 years in over 20 towns and cities, working with them to improve the results from their advertising. It has been a constant battle to get the best results on limited budgets.

Many small retailers have gone out of business in recent years because of rising costs and stiff opposition from large groups. Even large groups have had their problems, and many have had to rationalize their operations by closing uneconomic branches. Those retailers left in business today are fitter and more aggressive than they have been in the past.

This book is a do-it-yourself guide to retail advertising for men and women who are busy working. They have little time to spare for going on courses and little money to spare for paying advertising agents. It covers the basics of successful retail advertising, from planning to preparing effective advertising.

Open any local newspaper. You will usually find that the advertisements designed by advertising agents are superior to those drawn up by the retailers themselves. I hope through this book to help retailers to improve the effectiveness of their advertising, and to counter rising costs, increased competition and the ever-changing market. The cost of advertising has risen greatly and this makes it even more important that it should return the maximum sales for each pound spent.

Advertising agents may design better-looking advertisements and may not commit so many basic errors, but that does not mean that they can automatically get better results than retailers can on their own. Agents may know a lot about advertising, but retailers know a lot about retailing, selling, and, most important, their store and its merchandise. There is no magic in advertising; a retailer can easily pick up the rudiments that will ensure good results.

After 30 years I still see retailers producing the same type of advertisements, making the same mistakes and wasting valuable newspaper space that they have paid for. One of the reviewers of this typescript said that the advertisements chosen for illustration purposes were old-fashioned, and he was right. Fashions, styles and products themselves have changed over the years, but not the way in which they are presented in newspaper advertisements. All the examples chosen were taken from recent local newspapers, but that doesn't make them modern.

By looking at other retailers' advertisements it is easy to see ways to improve them, and it is hoped that the examples shown in this book will help you study your own advertising equally objectively. Some of the examples are from other countries, particularly America. This is inevitable in a book about retail advertising. America has for many years developed retail advertising quite separately from product or general advertising. Advertising is accepted as part of an agressive retailing scene in America and as a result it has produced many leading exponents in the art.

I am grateful to James Alexander of B.A.S.I.C., Bedell Advertising Sales Improvement Corporation, for his personal tuition many years ago, and for the help given to me by Tony Stroller, managing director of Radio 210, and David Fitzgerald and Co. Ltd.

I hope this book will be used as a basic reference manual by retailers who want to reduce some of the disadvantages of their position—and, still more important, to capitalize on their many advantages—compared with the chain stores.

1.

Why advertise?

A lot of muddled thinking goes on in retailer's minds over advertising. These are some typical examples: 'Everyone knows where we are!', 'Business is too good to advertise', 'Business is too bad to advertise', 'Marks and Spencer don't advertise, so why should we?' The undeniable fact that advertising is expensive raises other doubts. On top of all this, some retailers have confused feelings about their role in society, and even feel guilty about making a profit. After all isn't it popularly believed that to get rich you somehow have to be dishonest?

Everyone who becomes successful, let alone rich, becomes an object of envy, so even success poses problems.

This book is intended to be practical, not inspirational. Its aim is to tell you how to make your retail business successful through newspaper advertising. However, no amount of instruction will succeed unless you want to make advertising work. You need, above all, to have faith in it, and to take it up with enthusiasm. As this book progresses you will see that other qualities are called for too. Successful advertising is not a question of buying space or time and hoping that results will come from just 'putting your name in front of the public'. Successful advertising requires planning, imagination and a creative mind—three more success factors.

What is advertising?

Advertising is simply selling in print. For the mail-order company it literally means that prospects read the advertisement and are motivated to write a cheque, fill in an order form, and post them off to a company that may be hundreds of miles away. That's a big job for one advertisement, and often not a large advertisement at that.

1

It's known in the direct mail business as 'cash off the page'.

You, the retailer, have an advantage over a mail-order firm because your prospects can see before they buy, and you should get a greater response. So for a retailer selling in print means that your advertisement sells the idea that the public should come to your store to look at the merchandise you offer. At that stage you have prospects, not customers, and certainly not sales.

A retailer should regard advertising as an excellent leads system; it pulls out of the populace a number of prospects who hope they are going to find what they need in your store. Unlike the door-to-door salesman who makes many cold calls for each sale, you can count them as hot prospects. They become customers when negotiations begin, and sales when the transaction is complete.

Advertising is no more than a tool, a means by which you create store traffic.

The attitude of staff to advertising

Retail advertising cannot succeed alone; it needs to be supported with good face-to-face salesmanship by the store staff and with attractive in-store displays. The merchandise advertised should be on display in the store, presented in a manner befitting the star billing you gave it in your advertisement. We are in the self-selection age, and prospects expect to see before being asked to buy.

The salesperson, instead of saying rather ineptly 'Can I help you?', now has the opportunity to say 'That's the garment that was featured in our advertisement.' This opens the way for a more fruitful discussion and gives the prospect a chance to ask questions. When the first question is asked, negotiations have started and the prospect has become a customer. It's up to the salesperson to make that customer into a sale, but he or she has a head start because the prospect came in answer to an advertisement.

It is obvious that to succeed in a retail business that is advertising-led, you need enthusiasm throughout the store—a commitment from everyone involved, including the office staff or even your spouse if your business is a husband-and-wife operation.

Enthusiasm can be contagious and you can help to make it so. Don't save all your enthusiasm for your own ideas. Try to encourage a creative alliance with your staff. No person is motivated by money alone, and your sales staff will want to be recognized for the constructive part they play in the business. By holding regular staff meetings to discuss and plan promotions, considering carefully and acting upon staff suggestions if they are valid, you will get commitment and enthusiasm. Close the store for half an hour to show how important you think these meetings are.

The impact on profit

A store is a beautiful profit machine and advertising is the lubricant. Profit is the measure of the efficiency of that machine. Some years ago Her Majesty's Stationery Office published a booklet 'Gold in Your Hands', a useful document setting out the advantages of stock streamlining. It explained how a retailer could improve buying power by carrying fewer items in greater depth. Although it brought out the advantages of stock control, it never said how a retailer should let the outside world know of the dramatic changes that had been made to the store. An example of two retailers was used showing the difference to profit that an improved stock turn achieves. A similar exercise using advertising to ensure success illustrates the dramatic impact of advertising on profit.

Retailer A has £30 000 worth of stock at retail prices, and turns it over four times a year, giving an annual sales of £120 000. The gross profit margin is 25 per cent so the gross profit is £30 000. The store overheads come to £21 000, so this leaves Retailer A with £9000 net profit.

Retailer B, however, applies success principles and uses advertising as a sales tool. The value of B's stock is the same—£30 000—but because it turns over six times the annual sales are £180 000. The overheads are £21 000 because these costs remain more or less the same regardless of how much business the retailer does. B's gross profit was £45 000, but to achieve this 3 per cent (£5400) was spent on advertising. When this is added to the other costs, the overheads total £26 400, so the final net profit was £18 600 (proving that you don't have to double sales to double profit).

There are, of course, a few big retailers who don't advertise and yet seem to succeed. They succeed because all their other marketing elements are right and because they were established in less aggressive times. When they meet opposition that has the same marketing elements plus advertising, they run into difficulties. This was the case with Marks and Spencer in Canada, for example, where they are not a household name and the competition, which does advertise, is more aggressive. After discouraging results, they have had to start advertising themselves. In a newly developed category of business, such as DIY retailing, all the major retailers advertise.

Here is a case history. One Derby antique dealer had been in business for several years but his problem was getting antiques; he had waiting lists for many items. Dissatisfied with this state of affairs he decided to sell some new furniture and was pleasantly surprised at the response to his advertising. The next step was to take over an old warehouse and buy larger quantities of furniture. He took large advertisements, advertising immediate delivery—his turnover was so fast that he was receiving money before he paid his suppliers. His business had been transformed. Where he once was paying cash for secondhand furniture from the public, he was now buying on account from manufacturers. He claimed that his advertising was free because he had made his profit before he paid the newspaper. As if that were not enough, his part-exchange scheme opened up more doors to buying antiques than ever before. He was able to buy so many *chaise longues* that he could sell them to a southern buyer in the trade by the dozen.

Too many businesses believe the only road to profit to be by way of economies. If every possible economy in a store has been made and costs keep rising, the only way to increase profit is by increasing sales.

Objectives

The immediate objective of retail advertising is to sell merchandise. Only the very largest concerns can afford to buy advertising solely to promote an image. The average independent retailer is not in this position. In any case, the best way to project an image is through merchandise advertising; the public assess the image of the store by the quality of the merchandise and the manner in which it is presented in the advertisements.

Good advertising sells the goods *and* the store.

A marketing expression to note here is 'position in the marketplace'. In retailing terms having a position means that you have found and are serving a segment of the populace with the right merchandise in the right manner. This segment could be defined by demographics, age, sex, socio–economic factors, and so on or it may be defined by a common interest, such as sport, hobby, or parenthood, or even by a combination of interest and demographics.

All stores occupy a position somewhere in the marketplace. It is, therefore, important that the store's advertising matches that position. It could be, however, that you want or need to change it; to do so is not impossible, although this can be a difficult and painful process. When F. W. Woolworth, for instance, wished to shed the sixpenny- and threepenny-store image that had made them into a retailing giant, they hit the British public with a new image that proved unacceptable.

A credit draper in the Thames Valley ran a very successful business for many years and even in the late 1960s employed 200 or so part-time salesmen collectors; then new forms of credit, together with growing affluence, brought about the disappearance of the tally men. The business, which operated from a store of reasonable size, substantially increased its advertising in the hope of increasing cash sales. It worked. Customers came in large numbers and cash sales increased several fold—but the business failed. Sales did not equal the combined efforts of the tally men because the store was not equipped to cope with a rush of cash customers. There weren't, for example, enough tills, and, even more importantly, the staff weren't mentally prepared to deal with the cash customers.

A change in marketplace position is generally a question of evolution rather than revolution. Advertising acts as a catalyst and can quickly focus on the strengths and weaknesses of a store.

A good retail advertising plan involves every department every month of every year because all buyers are given advertising to sell their merchandise. This has several good side effects. Bad buying decisions are exposed when goods don't move despite good promotion. Faults in store layout are discovered when store traffic increases. Fast-selling lines stand out when they get the boost that advertising gives them. As a result management decisions are made sooner and more accurately.

Very often by listening to sales staff, a store can change direction on to a more profitable course. Their expert knowledge in a particular field may open up a new department. For example, a large toy retailer and wholesaler began life as a home improvement centre; toys were introduced just to boost the quiet weeks before Christmas. The marketplace became crowded with home improvement centres and, due to an over-reaction to a trough in the toy market, some competition in this area disappeared. It became obvious that the profitable course was to close the home improvement centre and to develop the toy side. That retailer lost a small home improvement centre, but gained a large toy business. Success follows expertise.

Suppose that your aggressive plan to increase your profits through advertising were to fail—where would you be? The answer is that even though you had spent money, you would be a lot further forward than if you hadn't advertised. You would have put your profit machine on a test run with the accelerator pressed further down than before. You would have sold more merchandise, discovered new talents, unearthed fast-selling lines and discovered the blemishes in the business. More people would know you exist and, hopefully, even if you didn't reach your profit goal, you would have increased your profitability.

Remember that Christopher Columbus failed—he was looking for a new route to India and discovered America, and that wasn't a bad alternative.

Advertising is expensive, but not too expensive to use—only too expensive to waste. This book will tell you how to use every centimeter wisely. The key is careful planning. Time must be devoted weekly to preparing each advertisement, monthly to each month's advertising plan, and annually to the plan for the year. Planning time is essential and a system will eliminate ambiguity.

Success factors

At this stage I hope that I have managed to clear away a few cobwebs and convince you that there is a strong case for advertising. Before moving on, look at the success factors that have so far been revealed as necessary if advertising is to yield optimum results.

1. *Belief* You need the knowledge that advertising can and will

work—not an empty statement, but an active faith that ensures that everything necessary to make it succeed will be done.

2. *Enthusiasm* This is the outer reflection of that inner belief, which will spread to all those who play a part in making the plan work.

3. *Planning* Advertising won't work unless you use a workable plan: more about this in the next chapter.

4. *Teamwork* Retail advertising will bring you prospects; you and your staff have to convert these into customers, and customers into sales. What is needed is a creative alliance between you and your staff or, if you are a small family business, an alliance between you and your family.

5. *Commitment* You need the commitment of the store staff to the success of your advertising-led sales plan. Secure this commitment by letting everyone have a say in the plan.

6. *See profit as a measure of efficiency* Profits climb faster than sales. Remember that you don't have to double sales to double net profit.

7. *Sell your store through your merchandise* Confine advertising to items for sale. Image comes across accurately from this type of advertising.

8. *Advertising exposes a store's strengths and weaknesses.*

9. *Don't anticipate failure from your advertising* If it should come it will probably be the type of failure that Christopher Columbus experienced.

10. *Advertising is only expensive if it doesn't work* Remember that many retailers are prepared to advertise in order not to lose their position in the marketplace. You may be prepared to defend your present income but, like Retailer B, *Are you prepared to double your income?*

2.

Planning your advertising

'It pays to advertise!' is a maxim that is old but true. 'Half the money spent on advertising is wasted—the problem is knowing which half', a statement attributed to a variety of business barons, is probably equally true.

The key to keeping waste to a minimum is to promote the right merchandise with the right amount of effort at the right time. Expensive advertising is the kind that doesn't bring a satisfactory return for every pound spent. Too many advertisers make the mistake of measuring the value of advertising by its cost rather than its results.

The biggest single advantage to planning retail advertising is that this enables every opportunity throughout the year to be matched with the right amount of sales effort. A good plan makes everyone in the store aware of the constant need to maintain a full head of selling steam. With costs rising at the rate they have been, there is a need to make receipts flow in with the same certainty as the bills for rates, lighting, heating, etc.

Unplanned advertising not only loses retail opportunities; it could ultimately harm a business by distorting its image. For example, take a high-class store that advertises only at sale time and spends advertising money two or three times a year on cut-price merchandise. Only those who know the store well know its quality. There is a danger that this advertising policy could result in a shift of position in the marketplace to compete disadvantageously with discounters who have greater skill in the discount business. A store should advertise the whole year round, when it is selling normal top-grade merchandise with a full mark-up, not just in the sale months. Planned advertising should present the true character and nature of the store, which involves representing every department, every month, according to its potential.

A good advertising-led sales plan gives buyers or department heads the responsibility of justifying the expenditure allocated to them each month. The plan also involves monitoring the results, department by department. The effect is to sharpen the store's total selling efforts, including in-store and window displays, by using advertising as the tool.

Profitable advertising uses a four-step plan.
1. Set a sales goal.
2. Decide how much advertising.
3. Decide what to promote.
4. Schedule the advertisements.

Check your sales pattern

This check is an important preliminary to the four-step plan outlined above. People buy to a predictable pattern. Figure 2.1 for

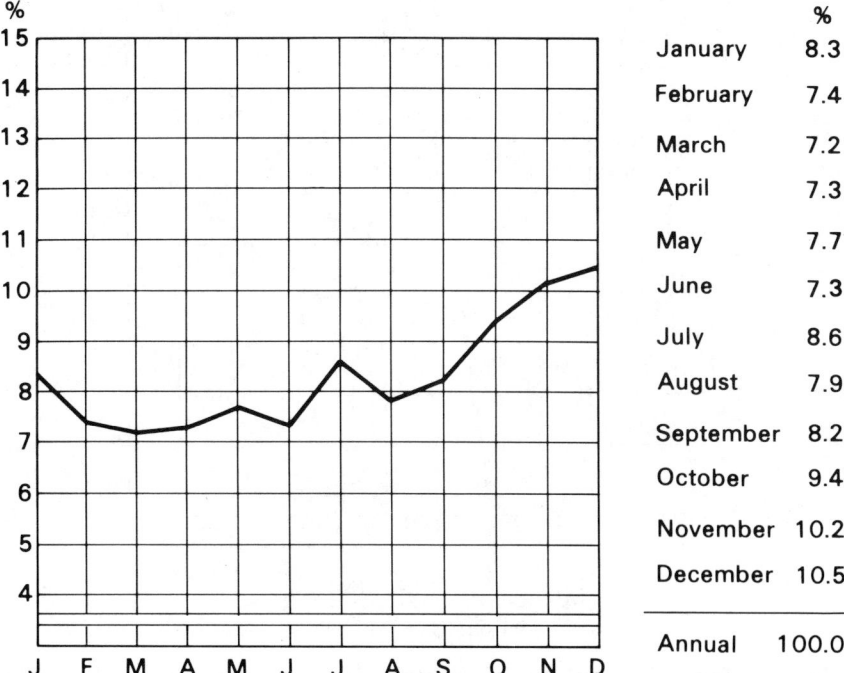

	%
January	8.3
February	7.4
March	7.2
April	7.3
May	7.7
June	7.3
July	8.6
August	7.9
September	8.2
October	9.4
November	10.2
December	10.5
Annual	100.0

Fig. 2.1 Store sales graph This graph is an average furniture store but the only sales pattern that matters is your own

example, shows the sales of an average furniture store, with each month's sales shown as a percentage of the annual total. No store, however, is average, and the only sales pattern that matters is that of your store.

Your sales pattern will have been formed over the years, according to the merchandise sold, the clientele, and the location, among many other factors. Each store is unique. Find your own sales pattern, and work out each month's sales as a percentage of the annual total.

Next plot your advertising month by month and see how it compares. Ideally it should follow the sales graph closely. Don't be surprised if the result looks instead like Fig. 2.2. This sort of advertising pattern reflects the belief that some months are not worth bothering about, while in others the strong promotional platform of

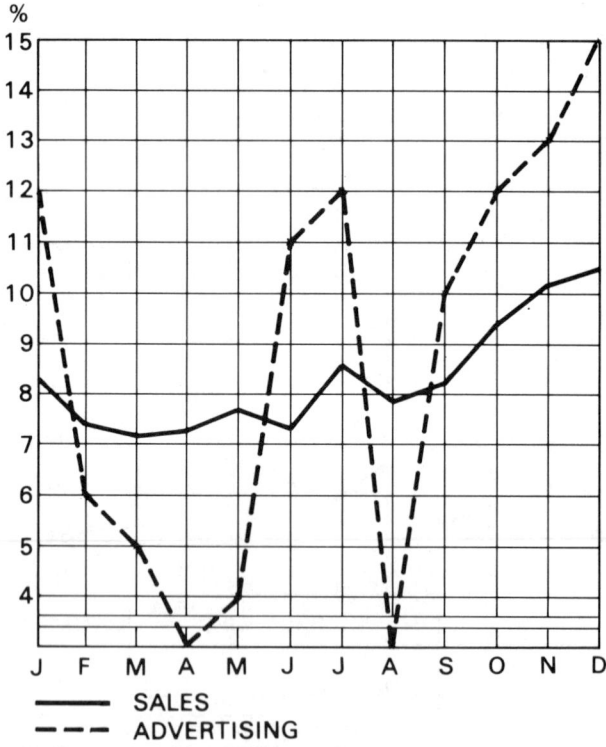

Fig. 2.2 **Sales in relation to advertising   Do not be surprised if your advertising graph looks different from the sales pattern. Good planning will make the two lines correlate**

a sale offers an opportunity to enthuse in print. Logically, if a store does 7.2 per cent of its business in March it should spend 7.2 per cent of its advertising budget in March, unless there are special reasons not to.

You can choose the last calendar year or the last 12 months for this exercise, by the way, or even the previous calendar year. It is surprising how little difference the choice makes for a well-established store.

Having seen how the appropriation is spread over the year, you now need to check that the right amount of advertising is being allocated to each department. Take a month of your choice from last year and calculate the percentage that each department or line contributed to the total sales in that month. Measure the advertising for each department or line taken during the same month, and convert this into percentages of the total month's advertising. Now compare the two columns of percentages. They should be similar; if they aren't, some departments are being promoted at the expense of others. If all departments get their appropriate share of the budget, the advertising will reflect more closely the true image of the store.

Set a sales goal

The first step in the plan is to set an annual sales goal to forecast what sales are expected. The starting point, as with any other sale projection, will probably be last year's turnover, adjusted upwards for various factors such as inflation, competition, extra promotion, expansion, and so on. If you are going to operate an advertising-led sales plan, you should add extra for that too.

The end product should be a sales goal that is optimistic but realistic. It is important to write down this sales goal and all the steps you intend to take to achieve it. Be bold and adventurous, but think through all the implications. Assuming that advertising can bring the prospects in, can you get the merchandise? Can you and your staff convert the prospects into customers?

This important first step in your plan requires deep thought. List the objectives that you need to achieve in order to succeed in reaching the sales goal. Here are some that you may have to include: a higher turnover per square foot of sales area floor space, a greater number of times turnover of the stock, a higher sales value per member of staff, more customers or a bigger transaction for each customer, or even both.

Is there any real reason why these objectives cannot be achieved? Writing down your sales goal and objectives fosters greater commitment from yourself and your staff.

Decide the advertising budget

Planning advertising expenditure is like any other aspect of budgetary control. Essentially it is just a matter of setting a limit to the amount to be spent, of deciding how much you are prepared to spend for a given return.

The amount to be spent, which should preferably be expressed as a percentage of the sales goal, needs to be determined by a number of factors: location of the store, competition, age and type of store, level of the sales goal, objectives and policies of the store, and many more. Not least important nowadays must be the pressure of profits created by rising costs, probably at a stage when every economy in overheads has been made. For most stores, the only way to higher net profits must be through more sales.

There is no hard and fast rule as to what percentage of the sales goal should be allocated to the advertising budget. Most advertisers operate in the 2 to 3 per cent region, but a few fall as low as 0.5 per cent or rise as high as 10 per cent. If your existing advertising is done only at obvious promotion platforms, the amount spent must increase to cover the neglected months. A discount operation like MFI used £6 million to secure a turnover of £100 million at a time when its competitors were shrinking in a recession. If your sales goal is ambitious, allow ample funds to achieve that goal. Do a profit check, assuming that your sales goal is reached and that you spend the amount you intend to. Is the profit going to be satisfactory? Remember that profits should climb faster than sales because of the fixed nature of overheads.

The coming year may bring unforeseen opportunities or promotions that were missed at the planning stage. To cover this, it is recommended that 10 per cent of your appropriation is set aside for a contingency fund. The remaining money should then be allocated monthly according to sales. For example, the furniture store in Fig.

2.1, whose sales goal is £250 000, decides to spend 5 per cent on advertising. It would have a total for the year of £12 500 broken down (to the nearest £1) as follows: Contingency fund £1250, January (8.3 per cent) £930, February (7.4 per cent) £829, March (7.2 per cent) £806, and so on.

Allocate the budget to each department

It is necessary to know what each department's sales are expected to be month by month. Your normal budgetary control or past trading figures may already show this.

Every department head needs to know the department's sales target and advertising allocation sufficiently far enough ahead to ensure that the right merchandise will be available and to put together an attractive offer. Store and window displays featuring the advertised merchandise will have to be organized.

Suppose the furniture store in Fig. 2.1 has six departments expected to make the following contributions to the store's total sales of £25 500 (10.2 per cent) in November:

	per cent		per cent
Bedroom	15	China and glass	25
Lounge	25	Carpets	10
Dining room	20	Kitchen	5

The £1147 monthly budget should be allocated in accordance with expected sales contributions as follows:

	£		£
Bedroom	172	China and glass	287
Lounge	287	Carpets	115
Dining room	229	Kitchen	57

This way every department has a share of the month's appropriation, and the advertisement readers get a comprehensive view of the store through the goods each department offers.

Schedule the advertisements

The next stage is to convert each department's allocation into newspaper advertising space. (There should also be some manufacturer's cooperative advertising to supplement the store budget but because the subject of cooperative advertising is of growing importance, it is dealt with separately in Chapter 9.)

At this stage we will deal with the retailer's own budget, continuing to use Fig. 2.1, the furniture store, as an example. For simplicity's sake we will assume that the furniture store's local newspaper charges £3 per single column centimetre. It follows that in November there are 382 centimetres to be scheduled. From local knowledge and the store's own records it should be possible to determine whether it is best to use four advertisements of more or less equal size or whether it might make sense to promote more one week than another, or even to put all the allocation into one advertisement. The latter course might be necessary if one were trying to counter a competitor or if a month's budget were being put into one store-wide promotion. If this were the case, however, it could be that the budget is just not big enough to do what you want it to.

Generally it pays to cover all weekends, and, therefore every selling opportunity. Logical groupings for four roughly equal weeks would be:

Week 1	Upholstery	96 cm	(32 cm × 3 columns)
Week 2	China and glass	96 cm	(32 cm × 3 columns)
Week 3	Kitchen	19 cm ⎱	(combined to fill
	Dining room	77 cm ⎰	32 cm × 3 columns)
Week 4	Bedroom furniture	57 cm ⎱	(combined to fill
	Carpets	39 cm ⎰	32 cm × 3 columns)

The total cost would be £1152, so only £5 would have to be drawn from the contingency fund, in return for achieving consistent shape and of advertisement size throughout the month.

Monitor the results

If there were to be a fifth step in the instructions, it would be to monitor the results. Any retailer adopting this advertising-led sales plan, knowing the objectives, will naturally want to check the results month by month or department by department and adjust the plan if necessary.

No store is too small to adopt this plan, not even the smallest husband-and-wife business to whom the mention of departments may sound grandiose. In fact, the smaller a business, the easier it is to administer and the further it has to grow. A furniture store has been used as an example but the principles are the same whatever the business.

No plan is a straightjacket—it can always be changed if a real need arises. Having a plan, however, ensures that you can cover every selling opportunity for every department every month. Most advertising brings store traffic, but this plan brings commitment from the staff and money in the till.

Success factors

1. *Commitment*   Everyone in the store is part of the plan. Every department should be committed to using and getting results from advertising every month.
2. *Support with display*   Make sure that advertised merchandise is displayed both in the store and in the windows.
3. *Check your sales pattern*   In a graph relate sales to advertising for the last year. They should match. Your sales pattern is important because your business is unique.
4. *Set a sales goal*   Be bold and adventurous but back up your target with a workable action plan in addition to the advertising plan.
5. *Decide an advertisement budget*   If your sales goal is daring, don't under-budget on advertisement expenditure. Check your profit plan for the store.
6. *Allocate the budget to each department*   Make an advertising allowance for each department according to its contribution to the month's sales goal.
7. *Schedule the advertisements*   Cover each week if possible but check your sales records in case some weeks offer better opportunities.
8. *Monitor the results*   Each advertisement should mean increased sales after publication. Keep an eye on the progress of the plan and if you are not reaching your sales goal, find out why.

Make a workable plan and make the plan work

3.

Words sell—headlines

Sometimes the mere repetition in a newspaper of a retailer's name and the nature of his business will bring results. The chance of this happening, however, shrinks as more and more sophisticated multiple retailers and discounters publish more and more compelling advertisements.

Sadly, many retailers publish advertisements that are old-fashioned, compiled in the simple belief that advertising is merely a question of attracting attention. Many more retailers behave in their advertisements in a manner quite uncharacteristic of their behaviour in business. A dignified store run by a respected, well-known figure in a local community may incongruously use a comic cartoon approach in advertising. A store occupying a trusted position within its community and selling top-quality merchandise may publish advertisements that emulate itinerant traders' announcements (not that there isn't often a strong sales technique in many itinerant traders' advertisements).

Advertising can often be improved by the addition of an illustration or a selling phrase or two.

There are five basic components of an advertisement: headline, selling copy, illustration, name and address, and white space. Here we will take a look at the first component and see how we can make it work harder to improve selling power.

Identify the prospect

The headline—those first few powerful well-chosen words that form the entrance to the advertisement—is vital to its success and must hit the interest of the right prospect like a well-aimed bullet. The right prospect is important, so the closer the headline can get to that prospect the better. If you are selling garden tools, for example, and want to attract the attention of gardeners or potential gardeners, you should use the words, 'garden', 'gardeners' or 'gardening' in the headline. Despite this, many retailers use a single word or brief phrase which may not even have any relevance to the full range of potential buyers.

There is a three-question formula to help find the right headline. The questions are 'Who?' 'What?' and 'Why?'

Who do I want to read this advertisement?
What do I want to offer them?
Why should they want to buy?

The first objective is to identify precisely those prospects you want to reach. It may not be close enough just to say 'men'; for instance, you may want to say 'large men' or, even more precisely, you may wish to reach men who are six feet or more tall, or 42 inches or more around the chest. Suppose that you specialize in outsize menswear and are capable of dressing the largest of men smartly. Your headline for an advertisement for tailored suits might read: 'Men over 6 feet tall or 42 inches or more around the chest can be the best-dressed men in town'. It's a long headline but it does select the right prospects and, almost equally important, precludes the non-prospects. The promised benefit of being smartly dressed ensures favourable attention.

A headline that tries to address everyone may not fail, but the headline that attracts the favourable attention of the largest number of the right kind of prospects will produce greater business.

Promise a benefit

Too many retailers assume that the only benefit likely to arouse customer interest is cost-cutting. Not so! There are many other reasons for buying—take, for example, beds, which are bought for comfort, appearance, size or even health, all of which are more important to the prospect than cost.

To find the right benefit, pick out the biggest single benefit of that particular item and build it into the headline—for example, 'Sleep better and awake refreshed with this comfortable bed'. Cost is a secondary benefit. Avoid the common mistake of using a single-word label headline like 'Beds', this restricts the advertisement's appeal to those who are in the market for a bed at that particular moment. The National Bedding Federation estimates that 15 million beds need replacing in the United Kingdom; at the same time, bad backs are this country's fastest growing medical problem. A bed advertisement should not only reach those in the immediate market for a new bed, but also those who with a little extra persuasion will buy. Those people may read the advertisement and be alerted to their need for a new bed.

A single word, like BEDS or the even more commonly used word SALE, is often chosen as a headline because it stands out. Graphically it is felt to be more desirable to use big type in short, bold headlines. There is no justification for this approach. Interested prospects will read long headlines, and long headlines help the advertisement even influence those who may not be in the market at that time.

Everyone has in their mind a list of wants and a list of needs. Advertising can move an item from the list of wants right to the top of the list of needs. We want many things, we need many things— but priorities dictate what we buy. The process of rearranging the prospect's priorities begins with the headline. While a word like BEDS is a mere label attracting only those who are currently looking for beds the word SALE on its own is too general. It shouts at everyone but tells no one anything helpful. At the very least some idea of what merchandise is being sold is necessary. The selling idea begins with the headline pointing out that the need is there and that the product can fill that need.

Get the message across

One of the most famous headlines of all time was written by Bill Caples, a copywriter who knew the power of professional selling in print. It said 'They laughed when I sat down at the piano, but when I started to play!' A total of 15 words, but it attracted the right kind of prospects in large numbers and was a winner for results, proving that impact is more than just the physical size of the type. The first consideration has always got to be the message. Graphics must serve the message, not the message serve the graphics.

Sometimes it pays to take a major objection and turn it to an advantage in the headline, promising a bigger benefit even than a discount. Take the case of two fencing advertisements. Figure 3.1 is offering special prices and is aimed solely at those who are in the market for buying new fencing and feel able to do the work themselves. It has many good points, but how much better the headline is in the example shown in Fig. 3.2. There the headline challenges a major objection, the 'do it yourself' problem, and promises a much bigger and more important benefit than 10 per cent off. It plants a buying idea with the suggestion that you can add value and beauty to your home easily.

Occasionally the offer is so big that the headline needs to spell it out loud and clear. Look through Sunday colour supplements to see examples. One firm offering a 36-piece dinner service together with 12 drinking glasses and 56 pieces of cutlery for less than £30 used, for example, the following headline: 'The names are famous. The price is unheard of. This complete 104-piece set for only £29.95'. This long headline was immediately followed by the entire 104 pieces clearly arranged in a photograph.

'Keeping your name before the public' is a concept that shrouds many inept practices in advertising, not least the common belief that it is desirable to put the advertiser's name at the top instead of a headline. This ignores the fact that the reader loves himself, not you. An advertisement must address the prospect, not the advertiser, and the prospect wants the promise of a benefit.

There are, however, occasions when the headline is enhanced by the addition of the advertiser's name—i.e., when the advertiser is an expert. Most specialist retailers are experts in their chosen field because the specialist retailer develops a knowledge about products that give the prospect buying confidence. Make the prospect aware that you are an expert. Even that wonderful headline in Fig. 3.2 would be improved if it had just a few additional words, if it said, for example, 'Master the art of fencing with the help of Buildall . . . and increase the value of your property'.

Verbs liven up headlines. They automatically use the 'you' concept. If you tell someone to do something, you are talking about them and not about yourself or your business. The Buildall advertisement used the word 'master' as a verb and therefore involves the prospect.

Fig. 3.1   Special prices are the sole attraction of this advertisement

Fig. 3.2   Plant a buying idea   This headline attracts a larger audience because it promises a reward for mastering the art of fencing

Adjectives in headlines can become hackneyed. The word 'exciting', for example, is overplayed. How much more stimulating it is to use verbs: 'Entertain your friends in comfort', 'Enjoy the luxury of . . .', 'Collect the antiques of tomorrow', and many more like 'Love', 'Behold', 'Revel' that would unlock a closed mind and start the acquisitive processes working.

Puns seldom work. Odd copywriters still use them but enthusiasm for puns in headlines has fortunately passed. They may occasionally raise a smile, but they frequently pass unnoticed and rarely sell.

Big stores and Omnibus headlines

So far this chapter has dealt with a retail advertisement for a single product or a single major product with related items, which is rifle shot advertising compared with the salvo that a larger store may require. (Incidentally, all big stores create a big store image quite rightly by grouping several departments' advertising space into one big advertisement.)

The omnibus advertisement requires a headline that embraces several departments. The broader appeal of a bigger store may lose some individual prospects for individual departments but the bigger general advertisement will generate greater store traffic and benefit all departments.

For the larger store, store traffic is important and promotions that link departments are important to create store excitement. You need in this case a headline that stresses the big benefits of shopping at your store. Ask yourself 'Why should people shop here?' or 'Why do people shop here?' Is it pride? Is it confidence? Reliability? Honesty? Service? A guarantee? Your uniqueness?

If you don't know why people should shop in your store, the question takes on a different significance. You will first need to rectify the situation by creating reasons for shopping in your store.

A store that has found its position in the marketplace knows what its customers want in the way of goods, service and terms. When you know these then you know the most productive benefits to headline.

A promotion overline is not a headline. You may have a campaign logotype for your event but you still need a headline selling the major benefit.

Finally, in large advertisements don't rely on one major headline; put in a subheadline for each department. Even the smallest subhead will be spotted by the right prospects if it is addressed to them and promises them a benefit.

Use news

Readers expect to find news in the newspaper, even in the advertisements, so if you can genuinely use the word 'news' or 'new' in an advertisement do so. Be like a reporter: view activities in a 'newshound' manner, the latest stock arrivals, store alterations, fashion trends, handy hints. In short, be topical. It all happens in your store if you are a boss who can make it happen. A new range arriving at the most important store in town, your store, is a newsworthy event.

Another headline technique is to provoke curiosity. To go back to the case of the outsize men's shop, still attracting the attention of the right prospect and still implying a benefit, the headline might read: 'Big men are dressing better'. This is sufficiently thought-provoking to make the prospect want to read on.

The closer to home you make a headline in every way the more effective it will be, closer not only in distance, by using the name of the town or newspaper, but closer in time by tying the headline to the season or the occasion, or even the day.

Success factors

1. *Identify your prospect* In the headline, aim the message at him or her, no one else.
2. *Promise a benefit* Do this in the headline and the prospect will read the body copy.
3. *Cost is not the only benefit* Use the biggest benefit the product has to offer to ensure the widest response. Cost saving may not be the right choice.
4. *Use as many words as necessary* Make the headline attract the favourable attention of the right prospects regardless of the number of words it takes.
5. *Graphics serve the message* The words of the advertisement are its most important element. Impact is gained from choice of

words, not size of type.

6. *Plant a selling idea*   Use your headline to sell the idea of buying to a wider audience than those in the immediate market for your wares.

7. *Expertise builds buying confidence*   Use your name in the headline with an air of authority if you specialize in your field.

8. *Verbs involve the prospect*   Add a verb and you add action.

9. *Omnibus advertisements*   Use omnibus headlines that broaden the appeal on wide-ranging merchandise advertisements. Ask yourself 'Why should people shop here?'

10. *Use subheads*   Advertisements covering more than one department need benefit-promising subheadlines for each department.

11. *Use news*   Be a 'newshound' in your own store. Look out for topical information to make news headlines. Your store is the most important one in town.

The first words are the most important words in a sale

4.

Creating the desire to buy

Having gained the favourable attention of the right prospect through the headline, your next step is to create the desire to buy. This brings us to the second component of an advertisement, the words that are going to convert the reader to a prospect, the selling copy.

Selling copy

The words are the most important part of a retail newspaper advertisement and yet often the most underrated. Just as in person-to-person selling careless words lose sales and well-chosen words make them, so it is in professional advertising. The difference between professional selling over the counter and professional selling in advertising is that in one case you are selling to an audience of one and in the other you are selling to thousands. Although you are selling to thousands, each individual reads the advertisement as if it were just for him or her.

Because advertisement copy is a monologue, the writer should have in mind a clear idea of the questions the prospective buyer might ask and write the copy to give enough information to clinch the sale. Every piece of merchandise has its selling points and its benefits and writing the copy is a matter of writing down the selling points and following or preceding it with the benefit. Let's take, for example, a bra and pick out the selling points such as style, material, colour and price. What can be said about the selling points? The bra is simple in design, made in nylon, trimmed with lace, costs £4.25 and made by Sunarama. We could assemble these selling points into copy with their relevant benefits as follows:

This bra is one of the latest designs now available from our special Spring range of underfashions. The silky smooth nylon will retain the moulding of your natural shape while giving the desired support. Lace trimming adds a gentle feminine touch. Styled by Sunarama, this enchanting bra costs only £4.25 and is available in cream, white and peach in five bust sizes (A, B and C cup). A small price to pay for confidence. Buy now while we have one in your size.

Not only does this copy convert each selling point into a benefit, it plants a buying seed in more readers' minds with its reference to confidence.

Selling points are either necessary for the product to function and fulfil its intended use or they are inherent in the manufacture of the product. For example, a product could be light in weight simply as a result of manufacturing it economically at a favourable price, but this same lightness in weight may make it easier to handle or carry, as in the case of garden furniture, luggage, lawn mowers, etc.

Whatever the selling points are, they should be listed along with their benefits and incorporated into the copy—the more benefits listed, the more likely the prospect is to buy. However, it is not necessary to list every single benefit; it may pay off to let the prospect 'discover' more benefits when visiting the store. But make sure your staff know the full range of benefits that the product has. This is part of the store's master plan, your creative alliance with the staff.

A list of benefits may not make the sale a certainty. Major resistances or objections may exist which the benefits are not big enough to outweigh. The proposed copy needs to be matched against a list of possible major objections that there might be to the purchase. The objections could be size, cost, time, inconvenience, incompatibility or many others, depending upon the product.

Read your copy from the right prospect's point of view—does it fill his or her needs and what are likely to be the objections?

The writer of the fencing advertisement (Fig. 3.2) thought carefully of the possible resistances and turned them into benefits. The first was the time or skill problem that a novice is likely to encounter because of not being a handyman. The second was the possibility that the prospect may feel that neighbours would regard the erection of a fence as unneighbourly. The first objection is challenged in the headline, and both are covered in the body copy as follows:

Good fences make good neighbours. They also increase the value of your home. A fence can add beauty and privacy to your garden area which makes any home that much more attractive. What a great way to make the most of outdoor living! Fences are a wise investment and it's easier than you think to build your own. Buildall can tell you how. Not only do we carry handy 'you really can' fencing guides—our selection of building materials is extensive. Just come in to Buildall and see for yourself! And our staff is noted for its friendly, knowledgeable service. No question you may have is too insignificant to be answered. Whether you're planning a fence, patio deck or just wanting to stain your picnic table, Buildall has the materials and advice you need.

May is the time to get to work on your outdoor projects. Buildall is the store to help you do it right.

This piece of excellent copy immediately enlarges upon the headlines, it gives benefits, overcomes possible objections, builds confidence and prompts action by a reminder that now is the time to do it. Each of the five items in the advertisement has benefit-promising copy.

Not only is selling needed for each item—no advertisement would be complete without copy to sell the store, suggesting all the reasons that make the store worth visiting. This means increased store traffic from the advertisement, not simply arising from those customers who are looking for the advertised lines. Each advertisement should pre-condition future prospects to believe that your store is the best place to shop.

Many retailers take a laconic view of advertising; the fewer words, the better. Is it because they fear that they may bore people? If so, they can rest assured that they won't bore **prospects**. Good advertising sorts prospects out from other people. It is, however, advisable to construct an advertisement that can be read either quickly by those who require little convincing or slowly by those who want more information. Cost might be presumed to be another argument for brevity, but display advertising is bought by the column centimetre, and most advertisements could contain extra words, both in the headline and body copy, without extra space and therefore extra cost. If pressure of space is a real problem, solve it by reducing the number of items advertised, eliminating the poorest sellers. The merchandise you advertise should in any case be your best sellers; promoting poor sellers lowers store traffic and weakens the store's image. No amount of advertising will sell a poor-selling line. After every advertisement, check your sales and don't repeat advertisements that haven't worked.

Prices

Have no qualms about quoting prices in an advertisement: they are a necessary selling point for the best results. For one thing, when prices are omitted the reader tends to assume that this is because they are high. The practice of not pricing goods in an advertisement, like not pricing them in the window, also presupposes that desire has been stimulated and once the prospect is in the store superior salesmanship will clinch the sale. Unfortunately this is rarely so. Few advertisements create that desire and even fewer sales staff are able to convert the prospect into a sale.

If an item is expensive, look for its unique selling points and spell out its extraordinary benefits. This way the impact of the cost is cushioned. Price is relative to a store's position in the marketplace anyway, and your prices will not come as a surprise to your prospects. Most retail advertisements draw the majority of their prospects from previous customers of the store, so its prices should be familiar to them.

A problem can arise, especially when prices are not competitive and advertising spotlights this weakness. In the long term, this is a problem that must be overcome. Fortunately, not everyone is searching for the lowest prices. Many people shop where they feel that they will get the kind of service they want or the credit they require. Store benefits are important for a retailer in this situation.

Conviction

However good an advertisement might be, its effect is weakened if it is not convincing. Conviction is a necessary ingredient for any retail advertisement. Without it, offers can be too good to be believed, a new product can sound so fantastic it can't be true, and quality is frequently doubted. Conviction should be reflected in all five components of the advertisement. In the selling copy, explanations build confidence.

A good word to remember and use in selling copy is 'because'. Why does the product do what it claims? Why are these goods so inexpensive? Ask the question from the reader's point of view. Your advertisement is an attempt through the one-way medium of print to have a two-way sales dialogue. Here is an example: 'This all-wool knitted jacket will keep you warm because it is made to retain your body warmth naturally.' This explanation reassures the reader as to the quality of the merchandise.

The same need to carry conviction applies when you are advertising low-priced goods. The reason for prices being low are many and varied—bulk purchase, stock clearance, imperfect goods and so on. The public believes that twice a year, at recognized times, a retailer must have a sale, but they will eventually lose faith in a 'continuous sale'. It is easier to accept, however, that one retailer has access to good-quality low-priced merchandise all the year round.

Many itinerant traders are sufficiently good at validating their 'sale' claims to convince a portion of the population of the genuineness of the event. One Welsh retailer used a similar technique in an advertising campaign for a sale at his own very permanent business address. It contained key elements that assured success. A full page on Thursday read as follows:

NOTE: Thomas Jones will be closed TOMORROW (Friday) till 12 noon, while they slash prices to provide you with tremendous savings.

This opening paragraph carried a lot of conviction because the store was actually closing while the staff altered price tickets. Then boldly, right across the page in big capital letters was the statement '20 HOURS ONLY'. This created a sense of urgency. Credibility was further enhanced with the following statement:

Frankly we are taking this drastic action to clear out huge assortments of odd pieces, discontinued styles, floor samples, surpluses of special purchases, cancellations, slightly damaged items. Hurry and find incredible bargains in this biggest ever WAREHOUSE CLEARANCE.

This was followed by reassurances as to the quality and a list of items and prices.

On Friday the page was repeated with minor alterations. On Saturday the advertisement was reduced to 36 centimetres across 6 columns and a bold sticker was placed across the top saying 'STOP PRESS . . . ENDS TOMORROW.'

The following week the 20-hour sale was repeated with similar announcements, but more words were added to explain why it was being repeated. This crucial explanation said:

ONE MORE TIME—We repeat this event in fairness to the great many people we were not able to wait on last week. We apologise! We will have more sales people this weekend—and we've added many more equivalent bargains to make this sale just as exciting.

This type of advertising matched the store's position in the market-place, a position most likely to be under attack from itinerant traders.

Whatever position you occupy within the marketplace, cut-price events need qualifying. Conviction comes with explanation. A specialist retailer should use in-depth knowledge of the business to provide explanations and details which reassure prospects (see Fig. 3.2). Never exaggerate. Let the actual goods be all you claim them to be—this way your advertising will be honest and the prospective buyer is not disappointed upon viewing the goods.

Latchlifters and sign-offs

Every advertisement offering a big ticket item should also carry a 'latchlifter' item, something small and low priced that the prospect can come in to see. It helps store traffic if people can expect also to make small cash purchases at the store.

One antique dealer used Rentokil as a 'latchlifter'. Anyone coming in for Rentokil was asked 'Have you got woodworm, then?' It wasn't long before part-exchanging the infected item was discussed and very often a sale was made.

Every advertisement should also sell the 'extra'—i.e., don't offer paint without brushes, beds without pillows, doors without knobs. Make the most of each transaction, and let the prospect know that he or she can 'one stop shop' for all the allied items.

End your copy with a call for action. Try to be timely, and avoid using the same sign-off line each time. Try to use urgency—e.g., '9 a.m. sharp', 'Ends tomorrow', 'Buy now and have it delivered in time for Christmas', 'Entirely new stock offered for the first time tomorrow', 'Call early and pick yourself a bargain', or (on a reassuring note) 'Call in tomorrow and see. You will not be pressed to buy'.

Getting ideas

Copywriting takes time but if you are working to an advertising plan it shouldn't mean a last-minute panic. It is also a good exercise for the sales staff and buyers to write the advertisement copy—who, after all, knows better than they the selling points and benefits of the merchandise? Make them full working members of your creative alliance.

Manufacturers' advertisements and brochures may also contain good selling copy but don't just accept it—top advertising agents are often guilty of not writing selling copy. To avoid the repetitious use of a few adjectives, have a good dictionary and *Roget's Thesaurus* to hand. Keep sentences short and words simple but use 'word magic', by writing from the readers' point of view and fulfilling their expectations.

Most sales people have the facts about the merchandise. More difficult but just as necessary is the ability to weave the dream that the readers want to buy. They want a guarantee, or the nearest thing to it, that the item will deliver that dream.

Prospects want reassurance, and they get it from knowing that the item is popular or in the case of expensive, exclusive lines, would be popular, price permitting. Reassurance also comes from knowing that the retailer himself uses or has used the same product: 'We tested it ourselves' is a powerfully reassuring statement.

If you are concerned about the length of copy, break it up into readable chunks with benefit-promising subheads. This makes an advertisement suitable for a fast read by those who do not need extra convincing; the longer read is for the undecided.

Finally, when you have written your copy, read it out loud and see if it makes sense from the prospect's point of view. Eliminate any superfluous wording that is not contributing to the sale.

For those who are interested in studying selling copy in more depth than I can devote to it here, I can recommend Clyde Bedell's *How to write advertising that sells* as a book worth reading.

Success factors

1. *Promote benefits*   Each selling point carries with it a benefit; spell the benefit out.
2. *Anticipate objections*   What are likely to be the resistances to this product or service? Provide the answer to these objections in your selling copy.
3. *Advertise best sellers*   Advertising makes best sellers sell even better, creates store traffic and boosts the store's image.
4. *Price-advertised merchandise*   If the goods are expensive, cushion the costs with bigger and better benefits.
5. *Add conviction*   By explaining why, what, or how, you build

confidence. Give reasons for special offers. Say why your store is the best place to shop.

6. *Provide the answers*   An advertisement is your attempt at a two-way sales-led conversation through the one-way medium of print. Think of the questions and provide the answers.

7. *Sell the extra*   Advertise small items with the main product to make each sale larger and demonstrate a one-stop shop service.

8. *Use of a latchlifter*   Offset a big ticket item with a low priced one to show people that they will find both small and large items in your store.

9. *Create urgency*   Finish with an 'action' line that makes the prospect feel that he or she must hurry before the best goes.

10. *Communicate clearly*   Speak the prospect's language. Keep sentences simple.

People buy for the benefit they will get from the product rather than for the product itself

5

Graphics serve the message

No display advertisement should be published without a picture unless a really suitable picture is impossible to obtain or use. Good advertisements are built around the words and the pictures should be used to illustrate the story.

There are many reasons for using illustrations but one of them is *not* that a picture saves words. A picture doesn't eliminate the need to explain in words, even at the risk of stating the obvious. Prospects are thirsty for information, verbal and pictorial.

An illustration, the third component of an advertisement, attracts attention. The right illustration attracts the attention of the right prospect—it supports the headline. An illustration also breaks up the copy, relieves the monotony of a mass of words and—if it's good—builds confidence.

There are three types of illustration. The first is an attention compellor, something that does not illustrate the product but is a device, often humorous to attract attention. Then there is product illustration, a plain straightforward picture of the item for sale. Finally there is 'product in use' illustration, a picture of the item for sale happily being used. This last is the best type of illustration because it allows the prospect to identify with the person featured in the advertisement—the woman wearing the dress, the man relaxing in his reclining chair, the family playing on the carpet. The product in use has a more persuasive effect than any other type of illustration because people buy a product for the benefit they hope they will derive from it. A picture of the product makes a good second best, and has the advantage of showing the prospect very clearly the features of the item advertised. Cost is a limiting factor, and for the small retailer getting the right illustration can be a problem—which has led to the establishment of a free illustration service by most newspapers. Their material is syndicated and the newspaper has bought the right to use it within its circulation area. From this service a regular supply of attention compellors is available.

Even large advertisers with advertising agents sometimes use attention compellors, but they may succeed only in paying a high price for an inferior illustration. An attention compellor needs to be relevant and to complement the headline. While all selling copy, especially advertising, should avoid being dull and serious and can even gain by exploiting humour, funny drawings need to be used with care. Advertising should match the image of the business.

There was a well-known case of an advertising agency that took a small account and wanted to do something exciting with it. The business was mail-order knitting machines and past advertising in appropriate women's magazines had been small, black-and-white, 'hard' selling advertisements with coupons. The agency used the entire year's budget in one full-colour, double-page spread using six models in off-beat poses for an attention compellor type of illustration. The headline read, 'You ain't seen knittin' yet!' The agency won an award for the advertisement, but it lost the account. The results were so poor and the advertisement so out of step with the image of the business that the client changed its agency.

The moral is to use humour with care.

Some manufacturers will pay something towards the costs of advertisements that feature their mechandise and many more will provide illustrations and photographs. One of the advantages of working to a plan is that you can often get the right illustration from your suppliers if you plan ahead. If you do this, however, bear in mind that the newspaper may insist on the artwork having a union label attached to it. Most manufacturers are aware of this and provide artwork that complies with this rule.

Photographs

Actual photographs carry more conviction than artist's drawings. The reader is more likely to be influenced by a photograph than by an artist's drawing, which he or she knows may contain some artist's licence. In the field of fashion this is less true. A woman may be influenced by an artist's line drawing. Perhaps a sketch conveys a sense of the fashion designer's exclusivity while photographs convey the impression of mass production.

There are many ways of imaginatively using a photograph apart from printing it square (see Fig. 5.1) as supplied. Naturally, unwanted parts can be trimmed off by straight trimming, but the entire background can be whitened out to allow the copy to flow around the illustration or the main feature to stand out in clear relief (see Fig. 5.2). Alternatively, part of the photograph can be square cut and part in relief, with the straight edge used to border the advertisement (Fig. 5.3).

Attractive effects can be obtained by mixing line illustration with halftone (photographs) in the same advertisement—it could be a photograph of the product with a line illustration from the newspaper's art service (Fig. 5.4).

The words of all advertisements should be legible, so avoid overprinting on photographs: insert a panel for the words instead (see Fig. 5.5). The inserted panel does not have to be square. As Fig. 5.6 shows, it can be round or even irregular, following the profile of the main feature.

There is an almost endless variety of ways to use photographs in advertisements but whatever the type of illustration—line drawing or photograph—use it as dominantly as possible. It should be an illustration that gives the advertisement its impact.

Reproducing photographs

There are two methods of printing newspapers: letterpress and the web offset lithographic process. The setting of the paper can be done by either of two processes: photo composition or the older hot metal system (now fast disappearing).

Photo composition and web offset require illustrations to be in the form of artwork, photographs or repro pulls, while hot metal printing requires a block or matrix of illustrations. Hot metal printing houses have the facilities (or access to them) for converting illustrations into blocks, but usually make an extra charge for this service.

Before an illustration can be reproduced in a newspaper, it is transferred several times from one surface to another until it is finally printed on the newsprint. For example, in a web offset process,

Fig. 5.1   Square-cut photograph   Unnecessary background has been trimmed off (Photo: Ian Pert, courtesy of the *Reading Evening Post*)

Fig. 5.2   Background removed   This is the same photograph with back-ground bleached out

Fig. 5.3   Part square cut, part bleached out In this instance the right-hand side is square cut to form the right-hand border of the advertisement

Fig. 5.4   Halftone combined with line   A bleached-out photograph with a line drawing from a newspaper illustration service by Adverkit International

Fig. 5.5   Square panel cut in for copy   Inserting a panel is preferable to overprinting copy on photographs

Fig. 5.6 Irregular panel Copy panels do not always have to be square cut; part of the figure or the product can be used for one side of the copy panel

the photograph or artwork you supply will be made into a bromide, which converts photographs into a series of dots. Black areas are made up of large dots and light areas of smaller dots, which produces the range of tones in a photograph. The bromide together with the rest of the advertisement is fitted into a paste-up of the entire newspaper page, a further negative is made, and the page printed onto a printing plate. On the press the printing plate transfers the image to a rubber blanket which in turn transfers the image to the newsprint.

In view of all these stages, it is hardly surprising that some loss of the original photograph's quality may occur by the time prospective customers see your merchandise in the newspaper.

The hot metal method is no better—in fact, its results may be worse because the essential printing dots have to be achieved on a zinc plate and after page make-up a cardboard mould (known by the printers as a flong) is made of the page. The final stage of this process is to cast a semi-cylindrical plate in a lead-based metal for printing directly onto the newsprint. Plain line drawings in simple black and white can withstand this chain of transfers better than photographs, but a line drawing may not carry the conviction of a photograph.

Newspaper printing is a black-and-white process, so the greys we see in photographs are an illusion, whichever method of printing is used. Each photograph is converted by the use of a screen of approximately 26 lines per centimetre. Your newspaper will use a standard screen for all photographs unless you say otherwise.

Within the constraints of the newspaper printing process there is a more than satisfactory method of reproducing illustrations that retain the authenticity of photographs and yet look like fine engravings. The secret lies in a photographic conversion process that breaks away from the regular dot image of the standard news photograph.

A popular conversion is mezzotint, an irregular screen process ideal for soft, tranquil subjects like the binocular case in Fig. 5.7. The binoculars are reproduced by a convincing, clean and precise process known as grey cut line.

Scrapertone (Fig. 5.8) is a semi-photographic technique pioneered by David Fitzgerald. It involves the transfer of a screened image onto

Fig. 5.7 Two conversion processes Mezzotint (the binoculars case) and grey cut line (the binoculars). (Process by David Fitzgerald and Company (Studio) Ltd, London)

scraperboard to which fine line work is added. It gives a product a distinctive, smooth, sleek appearance and retains a true-to-life photographic appeal. The processors require a longer deadline for this rather special process.

Black-and-white process costs vary depending upon the process used, but the cost is of little concern if the alternative is a photograph that does not enhance the merchandise or renders the product indistinguishable. For retail advertising, linear processing (Fig. 5.9) is popular because it is cost-effective and versatile enough

Fig. 5.8 Scrapertone   A semi-photographic technique that includes fine line work (Process by David Fitzgerald and Company (Studio) Ltd, London)

for a wide range of products. Some companies have not only genuine craftsmanship in black and white but also an enthusiasm for it. David Fitzgerald says 'It's our belief that black and white can have all the quality, depth and emotive pressure of good colour—given that it is used correctly'. The decision on which process is right for a particular product is one that requires expert knowledge.

Remember that every illustration in every advertisement should further the sale. If reproduction is likely to dissuade rather than persuade, it is better not to have an illustration at all.

Fig. 5.9   Linear is a cost-effective and versatile process suitable for retailers (Process by David Fitzgerald and Company (Studio) Ltd, London)

Illustrations aid perception

Sometimes virtually the same words in roughly the same space can be changed dramatically by the introduction of an illustration and a professional touch.

In Fig. 5.10, advertisement A is the copy of an inexperienced advertiser. The newspaper set the words just as they were written—no doubt the newspaper typesetter had found from experience that to change the wording supplied by an advertiser could result in refusal to pay for the advertisement. Even so, more thought should have gone into the setting and layout of this advertisement. Now look at advertisement B and see what a difference the use of an appropriate illustration makes. The shape was changed from a vertical 15 centimetre by two columns to a horizontal shape eight centimetres deep by four columns wide to accommodate the dynamic zip illustration. The priorities of the message have been sorted out: the words 'zip sale' together with the illustration which emphasizes the message, are allocated more than half the space.

Good artwork not only aids perception, when used dominantly it gives extra impact.

Assuming that you would prefer to use every single pound of

(a)

(b)

Fig. 5.10   An illustration aids perception   One dominant illustration not only gives more impact, it helps to sort out the message. Example B has the same words as A and only takes two column centimetres more space

your advertising budget on space in order to get the best value for your money, it is apparent that advance planning is important to secure illustrations from manufacturers. For the manufacturer the cost of high-quality artwork is more acceptable given his limited range of products and the entire range of printed media available.

Modern printing methods save block-making costs and even newspapers that do not have a modern press are under pressure to make blocks free of charge. Block-free printing processes make it easy to utilize artwork from other publications. This can be a boon where your supplier's material is concerned. Even so it is necessary to ask the supplier for permission to use it, in case there is any objection.

A retailer, particularly a small retailer, operating in a limited area and with a wide range of products to offer, cannot afford high production charges. This does not mean, however, that advertisements have to appear without illustration. All you need to do is think ahead and use some imagination to achieve good results.

There are occasions when graphics can tell a story far better than words. When competitors are promoting 'own label' and unknown brands, the store that is offering well-known brands has a good story to tell. The advertisement in Fig. 5.11 was 42 centimetres by two pages wide. A selection of popular food and non-food items are beautifully illustrated to substantiate the copy theme: 'Asda Price is Down. And not an unknown brand in sight. Just top name after top name like these.' Good art and neat type reflect the clean image of the store, and put over the message very forcefully.

There is another side to the picture, of course, giving an artist free licence to design an advertisement may produce an award-winning advertisement but no sales. Artists can get so carried away with design that they lose sight of important selling principles: the sales message is cut too short, names become unreadable, and even the product illustration disappears into artistic confusion.

Copyright

The copyright of any material used from the supplier belongs to the supplier or their agent. Equally, the copyright of any artwork that a retailer commissions belongs to the retailer. No other retailer can legally use artwork or illustrations that are your copyright without

Fig. 5.11   Bold art and neat type reflect the clean image of the store

getting your permission.

As you grow more successful, other retailers will want to copy your advertisements, but you can only prevent them making use of your actual artwork or typesetting. The words and ideas, unfortunately, are not covered by the copyright laws.

Success factors

1. *Every advertisement should have an illustration*   A picture helps the prospect in search of more information.
2. *Photographs build confidence*   The reader places more confidence

IS DOWN ASDA.

Asda Price is down. And not an unknown brand in sight. Just top name after top name like these, now made even lower than their previous low, low Asda Price. So make your way down to Asda and make extra savings now.

CHALFONT WAY, LOWER EARLEY DISTRICT CENTRE, READING. TEL: READING 83314

in photographs than drawings.

3. *An illustration finds the right prospect*   The right illustration supports the headline in its search for the right prospect.

4. *'Product in use' is the best illustration*   A picture of the product being happily used is the best type of illustration.

5. *Relevant illustration*   If you have to use an attention compellor, make sure it is relevant and complements the headline.

6. *Plan ahead*   By working to an advertising plan you can secure illustrations from your suppliers.

7. *Use photographs imaginatively*   There are many ways of using

photographs apart from the normal square-cut style.

8. *Don't overprint on photographs* Overprinting type onto halftones lessens legibility; cut a panel into the photograph for typesetting.

9. *Keep art costs down* Excessive artwork charges make inroads into your valuable advertising appropriation.

Expensively produced artwork can work to the detriment of sales

6.

Who is making this wonderful offer?

The right prospects' interest has been aroused, their desire stimulated, their doubts quelled, they are convinced. You asked for action and now you're going to get it: they are ready to buy.

Name, address and telephone number

The prospect's crucial last question is 'Who is making this wonderful offer and where do I find it?' If the selling story has been told properly people will read the smallest type to find your premises. Yet there are still advertising retailers who say, 'Everyone knows where I am!' The smaller the town, the more often a retailer is likely to make this rash assumption. Don't take chances: make it easy for people to find you. Always use the full name and address (component number four of the advertisement) including the street and the number. Draw a map if necessary. In this age of mobility, tell the readers where your store is in relation to nearby car parks.

There may be one or two details in the selling copy that a prospect needs to clarify before coming to the store, so include your telephone number. Incidentally, make sure your staff's sales training and briefing includes the person who answers the phone. If you are a big store, that includes the switchboard as well as the department extension. Just to test, go outside and ring your own store as a customer would and see if your telephone operator and department phone answering are as good as they should be.

Other useful information

Are you prepared to visit people's homes and offices to do business? If the answer is yes, say so in the advertisement.

Put in your hours of business to avoid frustrating your prospects.

Nothing could be more galling than to arouse the prospect's interest sufficiently to get him to your store only to find it closed and then shop elsewhere.

If you open later one morning a week for training purposes, tell the public and tell them the reason. It is good public relations to show that you care enough about your customers to train your staff to give better service.

Retail advertising is like face-to-face selling in that it depends upon attention to a lot of small details, the sum total of which ensures success.

Include credit facilities, and drop in the logotypes of the credit cards you handle. There is little point offering credit card facilities if these are not used to secure extra business.

When were you established? Ten years or more? If so, include the year you were established. It will distinguish your store plainly from any transient trader, and prove your record.

Logotype and type size

Every week your message and merchandise will change, but the name and address remains as a recurring element in your advertising. Endorse your identity by using the same name style, a logotype, each time you advertise. It should be a replica of the store sign and in the style used on vans and letterheaded paper. Apart from the obvious benefits of projecting a true image through the consistent use of the same logotype, there is less risk of printer's errors in telephone numbers and address if these are all on the same block.

An additional benefit from using a set block for the name and address is that it averts the problem of newspaper staff setting the sales message of the advertisement and using the name and address to fill the rest of the space. Rather than find themselves in an over-set situation, they will err on the side of undersetting the main copy.

Look again at Fig. 5.10. In advertisement A, space is wasted through symmetrical setting, and more than half the space is occupied by non-selling information like the name, address and hours of business. This information is important but not as important as the selling copy itself. The name in advertisement B is actually larger and moves to the bottom of the space; the hours of business are readable but condensed. There is only two column centimeters' difference between the two advertisements but apart from including an apt illustration, in advertisement B the words 'ZIP SALE' are much larger and the effect more dynamic.

If you don't have a logotype, at least be consistent. Once you are satisfied with the setting of your name and address, use actual newspaper cuttings of that set name style for future advertisements.

Apart from an urge to emblazon their name across the top of the advertisement, some advertisers also tend to set the name far too big. If the right merchandise has been selected and the advertisement is well designed and persuasively written, prospects will read the smallest size of print for the name and address. The best course is to make sure the size of the name is in proportion with the rest of the advertisement. As a rule, the space given to the name and address should not exceed 25 per cent of total advertisement area.

The majority of retail advertisements are answered by people who have shopped previously at the store. People prefer to shop where they have been satisfied in the past and they will read your advertisements for the news that they bring. However, there will be other readers who have never before used the store and may not even know where it is. This is new, possibly regular business; don't lose it by not letting them know where, when, and how to find you. When they have found you, make sure they are happy and they will read your future advertisements, because your merchandise and service have lived up to their promise.

Success factors

1. *Use your full name and address*   State clearly who and where you are. Don't lose a sale because the prospect couldn't find you.
2. *Use telephone numbers*   Put your telephone number in each advertisement for phone enquiries, but make sure the phones are manned by sales-conscious people.
3. *Use a logotype*   Use the same name style, preferably the one on the vans and letterheaded paper, every time you advertise. This reinforces your identity.
4. *Keep your name proportionate*   Don't waste space by having the name too large for the advertisement or by allowing the address

to spread over too great a depth.

5. *Provide extra information*   Make useful extra information a permanent part of the name and address block. Consider including car parking, credit facilities, hours of business, and possibly a map showing where you are.

6. *Show your permanence*   If you have been in business 10 years or more, state when you were established to avoid any idea that you are a transient business.

Good advertising is a collection of small sales points that lead to success

7.

A question of image

Every store is unique. Some of the reasons for your store's uniqueness are due to you, the proprietor, and some to factors outside your control.

The factors you can control are staff training and recruitment, buying and selling policies, and the type of service the store offers. Outside your control for your existing store are location within the town and the town's location within the country. You can't control what has happened in the past; your actions or your predecessors' actions helped place the store in its position in today's marketplace.

These factors and many more established the present clientele and advertising alone won't change it. Advertising is best used to develop the business within its established position in the market.

Advertising's second role is to reflect the true image of the store, however unique it may be, and there is no simple way to do this. An advertising image is built up from a lot of points, each in itself small and seemingly insignificant, but this is one of those cases where the whole is greater than the addition of the individual parts.

Getting the right advertising image for your store is not something you achieve with the first advertisement. Even the largest of companies with huge resources and extensive use of research adjust their advertising to match their image as they progress through an advertising programme.

With each advertisement you take, note the helpful features and retain them in future advertisements, but change the uncomplimentary elements, whether layout, type style, copy style, type of illustration, shape, size, or white space.

White space

The fifth and last component of the advertisement is white space—
it is the use of this within the frame of the advertisement that is a
key factor in projecting the image of the store.

Some advertisers are reluctant to pay for empty space; others feel
the copy shouldn't be cramped and are prepared to let the copy fill
the space loosely. Which view is right?

The advertiser who uses white space loosely is probably very
wrong, and the advertiser who packs the copy in tightly may be
right. It all depends upon the image of the business that you wish to
advertise.

If the business is a stocky kind of business—like a government
surplus shop, to take an example from one end of the scale—every
square centimetre of advertisement should be packed with items.
A good guide is the style of the window displays. If they are full of
items, like the typical government surplus store window, with small
items like boots, clasp knives and socks on the floor of the window
and outerwear on the back and sides and rucksacks around the top,
then that is how the advertisement should appear, side to side and
top to bottom filled with items.

If, on the other hand, the store were a high-class ladies' gown
shop whose windows are elegantly dressed with only one dress to a
window, then this store would be best using an uncluttered advertisement featuring a single garment. This way the advertisement
projects the same quality of image as the window, which is presumably the correct image of the store. Few retailers display their goods
in a manner that is out of keeping with the store—there seems to be
an instinctive dress sense for store display.

The advertisement's image is part of the prospect selection
process, and it is important for your advertisement to create a
favourable impression on the type and character of prospect that
you want to respond. The white space, or lack of it, is the advertisement component to which the prospect reacts subconsciously. If
it doesn't appeal, the eye is easily distracted by more interesting
matter on the page.

In many advertisements, white space is dissipated, allowed to
trickle between every line, down the sides, and round the illustration. The example shown in Fig. 7.1 wastes valuable space. The

BRIDGE STREET BUILDING SUPPLIES
49 - 50 BRIDGE STREET, TROEDYRHIW
Telephone: YNYSOWEN 690474

YOUNGMAN LADDERS PRE-SEASON SPECIAL!
3 - 6 metre WOODEN EXTENSION (20ft - 9in) £41.62
3 - 5 metre ALUMINIUM EXTENSION (20ft - 8in) £50.42
6 No. TREAD ALUMINIUM STEPS (6ft 6in) £21.20
LADDALOK STEPS 5ft 0in £17.20
(aluminium steps also available)

COPPER TUBE SPECIAL
3 metres (10ft 0in approx.) 28mm £4.34
3 metres (10ft 0in approx.) 22mm £3.07
3 metres (10ft 0in approx.) 15mm £1.66
Plus Full Range of Fitting at Discount Prices

MYSON RADIATORS — 35% OFF LIST
TIMBER AND DOORS SPECIAL
PAT. 10 2 x G and 2 x GG — Internal and External
Hardwood Quality — All Sizes £18.00
Carolina, Kentucky, Etc. — Also in stock

TIMBER EXAMPLES (Sawn):
3 x 2 — 10p per ft; 6 x 2 — 20p per ft; 7 x 2 — 24p per ft.
2 x 1 R/Batten — 3½p per ft.

STANDARD STAIRS SPECIAL:
32¼% DISCOUNT — Normally £122.84
Now Sells at £82.84

All Price above exclusive of V.A.T.
CHECK THESE PRICES AGAINST THE BIG LOCAL D.I.Y's
— that big is not always beautiful —
THERE IS ALSO NO HIDDEN DELIVERY CHARGE!
AGENTS FOR VENTOLUX PURPOSE MADE ROLLER SHUTTER,
VENETIAN AND VERTICAL BLINDS

Fig. 7.1 Valuable space dissipated The setting of this advertisement wastes 22 per cent of the printing area

copy is extended to fill three column widths with the use of dots or empty space down the sides of the items. Its layout is an uncomfortable mixture of the symmetrical and the asymmetrical, because part of it starts at the left and part is centred. The image this retailer wishes to project is no doubt that of a well-stocked practical builder's merchant; to that end the typeface conveys practicality and the number of products mentioned is a good attempt to convey the wide range of stock.

However, no less than 22 per cent of the advertisement's space is wasted. Without reducing any of the type sizes the copy could be rearranged as in Fig. 7.2, to leave two impressive blocks of white space that would help lift this advertisement from the rest of the page. Alternatively, the retailer could have taken a smaller space; instead of a 15 centimetre by three column advertisement, the same message using the same size of type could have been accommo-

BRIDGE STREET BUILDING SUPPLIES

49 – 50 BRIDGE STREET, TROEDYRHIW   Tel : YNYSOWEN 690474

YOUNGMAN LADDERS
PRE-SEASON SPECIAL

3 – 6 metre WOODEN EXTENSION (20ft·9in)	£41.62
3 – 5 metre ALUMINIUM EXTENSION (20ft·8in)	£50.42
6 No. TREAD ALUMINIUM STEPS (6ft 6in)	£21.20
LADDALOK STEPS 5ft 0in .	£17.20

COPPER TUBE SPECIAL

FULL RANGE OF FITTINGS AT DISCOUNT PRICES

3 metres (10ft 0in approx) 28mm	£4.84
3 metres (10ft 0in approx) 22mm	£3.07
3 metres (10ft 0in approx) 15mm	£1.68

MYSON RADIATORS- 35% OFF LIST

TIMBER AND DOORS SPECIAL

PAT. 102 x G and 2 x GG – Internal and External
Hardwood Quality -- All Sizes £18.00
Carolina, Kentucky, Etc. – Also in stock

TIMBER EXAMPLES (SAWN):

3 x 2 – 10p per ft; 6 x 2 – 20p per ft; 7 x 2 – 24p per ft.
2 x 1 R/Batten – 3½p per ft.

STANDARD STAIRS SPECIAL:

32½% DISCOUNT – £82.84

Normally £122.84

All Prices above exclusive of V.A.T.

CHECK THESE PRICES AGAINST THE BIG LOCAL D.I.Y's

—that big is not always beautiful—
THERE IS ALSO NO HIDDEN DELIVERY CHARGE!
AGENTS FOR VENTOLUX PURPOSE MADE ROLLER SHUTTER,
VENETIAN AND VERTICAL BLINDS

Fig. 7.2   Use white space in blocks without reducing the size of type. The type and white space are massed for better effect, but ideally the space could have been used for illustrations or more selling copy

dated in a 17 centimetre by two column advertisement. As in Fig. 7.1, valuable space has been frittered away, space that might have been used to put in more items, to put in a real headline, to put in illustrations, to put in hours of business and credit facilities, or to increase selling copy both for the merchandise and the store. The promise of a benefit, a hint as to the prospect's identity, and a guide to the retailer's position in the marketplace are all buried at the bottom of the frame. In fact, instead of being too big this advertisement is too small.

Wastage of valuable space often occurs as a result of sending the advertisement in without a working layout. To do a full type mark-up on an advertisement layout is a skilled job, but it is possible to present a layout to the printers showing where you would like the type and other components of the advertisement to go, as in Fig. 7.3.

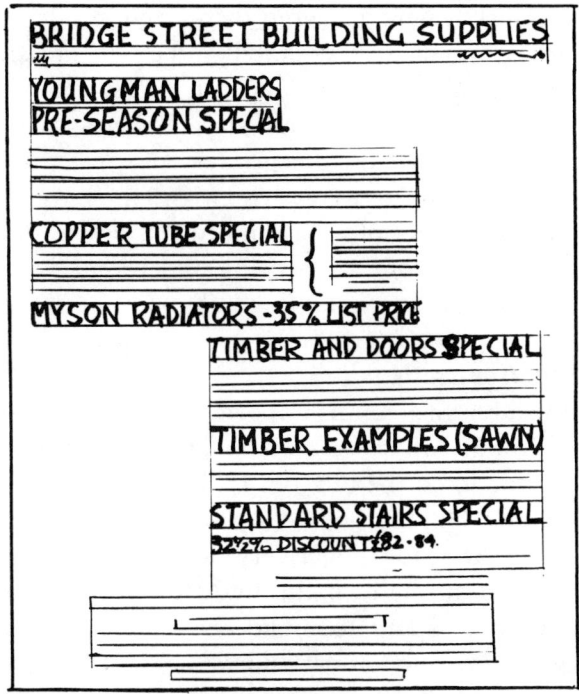

Fig. 7.3 A layout for the printers   Send your sample rough layout showing how you would like the advertisement to be set

Each advertisement you take should get you nearer to your ideal goal. After the publication of every advertisement, hold a discussion with the newspaper representative to make sure that your typesetting requirements are being heeded. It is important to achieve consistency through all your advertising, so once you are sure your typography reflects the store image, don't change it.

All elements of the advertisement should be consistent—the logotype, naturally, and also the shape (it needn't be the same size, just the same proportions). The type, the layout, the illustrations and the character of the copy should always echo the style of previous advertisements. Research has shown that a consistent look has a better impact on the prospective market. Hence, even the typeface of the advertisement should be chosen to conform to the same image. Use a light elegant type for an elegant store, a heavier type for the store that majors on practicality. Thick black heavy types are for scrap dealers, so avoid them even at sale times.

Whatever type you choose, stick to it and use it consistently, even to the extent of employing it throughout the store on tickets and showcards. The character of your store belongs to the store; it should not be dependent on the printer who sets the newspaper advertisements or the ticket writer who writes the store tickets. Even if you haven't the funds of a big multiple store to develop your identity you can give your advertising and promotional activities the stamp of individuality and sell merchandise at the same time.

Size of advertisement

The size of the advertisement is important. Big advertisements suggest a big store but, whatever size the store is, the advertisement must be adequate to do the full job. It should be big enough to get in a long headline, lengthy body copy, an illustration, white space, and a full name and address. Every advertisement must feature merchandise and especially if the budget is limited, there is not likely to be cash to spare to make non-selling statements or to embark upon 'image only' advertising.

Advertising bought for the reason of the lowest cost rather than the greatest benefit is bound to misfire. The right merchandise with the right message is paramount. None of the principles of good advertising should be sacrificed for cost. If an advertisement is too expensive, check that you have eliminated poor sellers but make sure you are selling good sellers really hard. This develops the store's strengths and a good but true image comes from this proven success system. If space costs are the problem, then frequency must be sacrificed in favour of size. The worst possible outcome is to put a poor-selling message starved of words with a low-grade image into mediocre-sized space.

Local newspapers carry many brief advertisements in spaces too big for the words. In order to economize, the advertiser buys a small space and makes the assumption that this calls for a brief message, rather like sending a telegram. The next mistake is to try to compensate for the brevity by using the largest possible typeface the limited space allows. The end result is an advertisement that is too small to include all selling elements and convey the correct image of the business.

Display advertisements on the news pages of the newspapers are advertisements that are looking for prospects, and you can't do that without merchandise and a message that appeals to the waverers as well as to the hot prospects. Alternatively, if you are satisfied with something less than selling to the widest possible audience and you don't feel that store image is important, then make the space smaller, put the advertisement into the classified columns of the newspaper, and enjoy the benefit of more frequent exposure. In the classified section of the newspaper your advertisement will be read by the prospects who are looking for advertisements. They are scanning the columns for genuine money-saving offers or services.

Copy and image

Merely publishing the name and address of the company together with the nature of the business will no doubt produce some results, but this is due solely to the multiplication by the media rather than the quality of the message.

In Fig. 7.4 the advertisement addresses only the limited number of people who are currently looking for garden paving, walling, fencing or patio doors. They are not promised any benefit, so there is no 'sell' in the advertisement and it does not reflect the company's image. It leads with a telephone number, but doesn't say why you should phone. Is it that you can order by phone? Or will they send a representative? Or will they send brochures?

The advertisement makes excessive use of capital letters and reverse white on black. Furthermore, it lacks a headline that contains a selling idea and body copy that persuades. A suitable headline that embraces the four products mentioned in the advertisement might be 'Extend your home now for great outdoor living', followed by the lead-in line, 'Enjoy summer days on your own patio with the help of Erith'. Together these would convey to the reader the impression of an expert company.

The follow-on copy needs to develop the headline theme and continue selling the idea:

A patio can make your home so much more attractive and at the same time increase the value of your property. What a great way to make the most of outdoor living. Erith have everything to make your patio a source of pleasure and yet private. Doing it yourself is easier than you think with Erith's expert advice. No question you may ask is too insigni-

Fig. 7.4   Black and bold is not a selling message   This advertisement lacks sales energy and does not reflect the company's image

ficant to answer. We also have a pamphlet on how to do it yourself or we can recommend a builder to do the job.

April is the month to make this investment, so that you can enjoy every day of summer. Why not come in to see our range of patio doors, fences, paving slabs and building blocks tomorrow? Our friendly, knowledgeable staff will help you to make a good job.

Each of the products then needs selling copy, even concrete products. The product points need to be unearthed and the benefits extolled, even if they are no different from any other maker's product. The selling points of a paving slab may be the 'mix', the size range, the colours, the surface, the price, and probably many other things that you, the expert, know about. Each of these selling points supports a benefit, (the mix gives the strength, the sizes give the weight for ease of handling and versatility, etc.). The selling points and benefits need to be woven into a sales story as follows:

Erith paving slabs are made from hard-wearing concrete that has been carefully mixed to avoid cracking and to maintain a pleasant restful colour through all weathers. The rectangular designs come in four sizes for ease of handling and maximum versatility. We have taken our lead from nature in the choice of colours, slate grey, Cumberland green, sandstone yellow, terracotta pink and natural York. Children can play safely on this paving because the surface is non-slip even when wet. They are safer than real stone but only a fraction of the cost.

This should be followed by the items and the prices.

The Erith advertisement was 20 centimetres deep by three columns wide and it would have been possible to print all the above copy, the headline, the subheadline, five items with copy plus an illustration of a family relaxing on a patio in that size of space. Apart from the improved selling job that such an advertisement would accomplish it would create the aura of an expert, knowledgeable company that cares about its products and customers.

Borders

How do you make your advertisement stand out from the rest in the newspaper? The answer is not to have a border so thick that it is a barrier. Some advertisers prefer to let the newspaper's dividing column rules separate their advertisements. The theory is to let the eye into the advertisement rather than to stop the message going out.

Only advertisements that go right across the page or completely from top to bottom of the page can manage without a border so choose one and stick to it. Make the border part of the store's advertising identity and, again, make it match the image of the store—an elegant border for an elegant store, a square-cut practical border for a practical store—but never let the border be so dominant that it swamps the message.

Image devices

Slogans, trade marks, and cartoon characters are the well-known devices that advertisers use to personify product or corporate identity to the public. Many are successful and become famous throughout the country, if not the world, either through years of use or an expensive advertising campaign.

The cartoon character is often an integral part of the advertising campaigns of a single product or service like British Telecom's Buzby, the Bisto Kids, Mr Therm or Tate and Lyle's Mr Cube. Similarly, the greatest slogans that spring to mind are those associated with a single product, like 'Double Diamond works wonders', for example. However, there is no reason why cartoon characters or a slogan should not enhance the regular advertising of a retailer.

Cartoon characters—unlike serious illustrative motifs—are only appropriate for certain businesses. Dairies, bakers and fast food shops, for example, can and do use plump, clean, smiling little men in their advertisements. Higher up the catering scale, a high-class restaurant for instance, the use of cheap and cheerful little men could be out of character to the type of clientele. Selling should be fun, fun that spills over into the advertising, but not at the expense of business credibility.

One can imagine the use of a cartoon in a handyman's shop advertising being acceptable, where the socio–economic profile of the clientele is of no significance and each customer at the weekend slips into the temporary role of builder, joiner or painter. A little 'Mr Fixit' type cartoon character would emphasize the bond between supplier and user. Cartoons should only be used if they are apt and match the character of the business.

Trade marks ought to convey the essence of the business and be memorable. If the trade mark is made from the company's initials,

pleasing you is important at John Martins

A few months ago we did a stocktaking. Not a normal kind of stocktaking, far from it. We took a good long look at ourselves, and how we related to you, the customer.

And what we saw didn't please us. Somehow, we'd <u>become complacent</u>! We had to do something about it.

From that moment on things began to happen in our store. At first it was almost indiscernible, like a gentle breeze wafting quietly from floor to floor, department to department. But with each day this new feeling of dedication grew in momentum till suddenly it had become an exhilarating storm of enthusiasm, and we were on our way.

Everybody seemed to get in on the act. Ideas came thick and fast. Good ideas. Brilliant ideas. Crazy ideas. Adventurous ideas. And we took them all, and sifted them out, and there was much burning of the midnight oil.

But it was worth it. From out of those ideas we came up with a new, and stronger policy of service for John Martins.

We'd care more about every customer. We'd try harder than we'd ever tried before, so much so that we'd have customers actually commenting on our excellent service. We'd have a bigger variety of new and different things to sell. And whether we were selling safety pins, refrigerators or fur coats, we'd go out of our way to be friendlier and more efficient. We determined to give you what would please you most in a department store.

Ambitious? Of course it is. And we're not perfect yet, we have a long way to go. But the enthusiasm is there. We can feel it right through the store. We hope you will too, because pleasing you is what it's all about!

pleasing you is important

John Martin's
OF SOUTH AUSTRALIA

Fig. 7.5 Establishing a slogan This was the first advertisement in a campaign that involved the whole store staff

they should not be so distorted that the symbol is meaningless and the initials unidentifiable.

The favourite repetitive device among retail advertisers is a slogan, a simple one-line statement that should convey the philosophy

Fig. 7.6 Continuing use of a theme   Subsequent merchandise advertisements carried the same slogan

of the store. If you can't summarize your store's philosophy in one line, don't force it. It is doubtful whether you could successfully steal someone else's slogan—slogans should be tailor-made, and they shouldn't be written if they're not true.

A slogan used for a campaign, however, may be found to fit for all time. Take the case of John Martins of South Australia, who ran a campaign called 'Pleasing you is important'. After the initial policy statement advertisement (Fig. 7.5) the theme followed through on institutional gift and summer merchandise advertising (Fig. 7.6). This campaign made a statement that the entire store staff had to live up to; it called for a creative alliance throughout the store.

To describe the unique position of a store in the marketplace is difficult if not impossible. At an interview in New York, Grace Perez Quiliano, sales promotion director of Bonwit Teller, was asked to describe the store's image. Here is her reply:

> Bonwit Teller is a very feminine store and it caters for the woman who really loves clothes. We cater to the woman who loves fashion. We don't run a lot of big promotions but we run intimate promotions because our customers like that kind of intimacy rather than large crowds. We don't attract that kind of customer. We have breakfast fashion shows, luncheons and lectures.
>
> We don't usually use a big headline in our advertisements, but we do include the product's benefits in the body copy, which is editorial and to the point. Our photographs are clear and the copy is concise, all ads include the phone number of the store as well as our other locations.
>
> The colours of the new store are mostly peach. Everything looks three dimensional. The lighting is very soft and it makes you feel like you are in a very feminine type of store. That's what I believe makes it different. It's very intimate. I think the store is very slick, and it's a very 'eighties store.

Miss Quiliano's description was a good attempt to put the store's image, which she knows so well, into words, but for the individual retailer it is probably a matter of instinct rather than precise knowledge.

Position in the marketplace

Established retailers instinctively know the class and type of customers who use their store and automatically adapt their selling techniques and strategies to match that position in the marketplace. The factors that position a store in the marketplace take many forms.

Each store is unique. For most, even the largest, its position is the result of evolution from small beginnings. Its position today depends upon the unique combination of:

1. Merchandise diversity.
2. Store size.
3. Range and age of customers.
4. Pricing policy.
5. Convenience (location, hours, ability to shop quickly).
6. Service (selling, delivery, after sales service).
7. Innovation (first with new ideas, a leader of fashion).

8. Lifestyle (age, interest, homes of customers).
9. Dependability (store's reputation).
10. Community identification (local store or chain store).

If strategy is seen in this light, why not make the advertising follow the same line? After all, the store displays are probably in tune.

Success factors

1. *Reflect store image*   Advertising should reflect the true image of the store. Only careful attention to many small points will achieve the correct portrayal of the store's character.

2. *Build consistency*   Each advertisement is a question of trial and error. When an element reflects your store's character, retain it through all future advertisements.

3. *Match your window displays*   Make your newspaper advertisements match your window displays in style and character.

4. *Style selects right prospects*   The advertisement's portrayal of your store's image is part of the prospect selection process. Style of advertisement affects the subconscious mind of your prospect.

5. *Treasure every centimetre*   Every centimetre of space that you use should be treasured. If a full advertisement is required, fill it with useful information and items, don't fritter the space away with untidy setting.

6. *White space for impact*   Use white space in noticeable masses. Use it to contrast blocks of type.

7. *Consistency throughout*   Be consistent with the name-style character of the copywriting, shape, layout, use of illustrations and typefaces, even to making them match the showcards and posters within your store.

8. *Merchandise projects the real image of a store*   A true store image comes from the merchandise you feature in your advertisement.

9. *Right size of advertisement*   Buy your advertising with a view to the greatest benefit to your sales objectives rather than for the lowest cost. Smaller advertisements can create a greater wastage than big ones.

10. *Same border every time*   Choose a border and use it every time. Let it match your image but not swamp the message.

11. *Symbol must be apt*   Use a symbol in all advertisements but make sure it is apt, simple, and matches your store's image.
12. *Slogans must be true*   Use a slogan but make sure it is individual, a one-line summary of the store's principal philosophy.

8.

Make every single day exciting

Most advertisers have no problems filling their advertising space at the time of a winter or summer sale. Advertisements are packed with items, sometimes almost indiscriminately, as department heads clamour for space. There are lines to clear for both retailer and manufacturer and in the sales fever special purchases are made by retailers to swell the 'take'. On the other hand, there are months when it is difficult to raise much enthusiasm for promoting sales. Despite this, statistics show that there is no month when sales are so slow that promotion isn't worth while. It therefore pays the aggressive retailer to promote every month of the year, if not every week, and make every single business day exciting.

Promoting every month does not mean jumping from one sale or cut-price bargain event to another. Within the full year's promotion calendar there should be a variety of promotions, most of which give the opportunity to reflect the quality of the store.

In difficult times many stores tend to press the panic button in an attempt to make short-term sales, even if it means sacrificing the image of the store. The key task is to maintain an excitement throughout the store for as many days of the year as possible, starting from the January sale.

Two sales a year

There are two accepted sale periods in the year. Make the most of each if it is your store's policy to have a sale. Start as early and finish as late as possible. The January sales, for example, can start before Christmas, as soon as it is too late to promise delivery for Christmas for the majority of big items.

Credibility is important in a sale, so even within the accepted genuine clearance periods it helps to provide a little extra 'evidence'. It can pay, for instance, to close the store for the day before the sale starts for the purpose of pricing the sale goods. This plan works best if your advertising medium is an evening newspaper and you are able to place an advertisement on two consecutive evenings. The first advertisement announces the all-day closing and gives the reason: that all price tickets are being altered that day, downwards.

The best day of the sale for takings is often the first; this will be a good day even if it is not a Saturday, so it is advantageous to start on a weekday and get a second impact on the first Saturday. In these circumstances, you might end up taking three advertisements in the first week of the event. If you are working to an advertising plan there will be a budget for the sale, and coverage for each week of the sale will have been determined long before the event. Each department's space allocation can then be decided in advance. This procedure charges every department head with the discipline of selecting the right merchandise to fill the space. It could mean cutting out indifferent items or it could mean finding good buys to justify a space allocation.

Sales lose their freshness as they proceed and as a result the response may decline. In view of this, it is essential for the advertising to maintain its appeal. Only once in a sale can the words 'Starts tomorrow' be used, but the word 'tomorrow' can be used in every advertisement. For example, you might say 'Bargains for you tomorrow' or a similar phrase. Avoid tired cliches like 'Sale now proceeding' or even, 'Now in full swing'.

Savings are the benefit the customer expects from a sale, so savings should be mentioned in the headline. It is never safe to assume that the public know what you sell, so in every advertisement make sure that the right prospect knows at a glance what goods are being offered.

When the sale is nearing its final stages there are lots of ruses to maintain maximum interest to the very end even if, in the case of the winter sale, that end may stretch well into February. You should only say 'Last few days' once, not for several weeks. It is better to be positive and urgent: 'Last week', 'Last three days', or 'Last day'. There is no reason why the following week the sale shouldn't change to another promotion.

The final clearance can be in many forms. One example is the 'Red tag clearance', in which the advertisement explains that certain unsold merchandise will be given a final price on a special red swing ticket. Similarly, on 'Blue cross days', the sale price is crossed out in blue crayon and the final price written in. 'Rainbow savings', where final percentage reductions are indicated with a different coloured ticket, are another possibility. These three examples are better if the newspaper can use spot colour to echo the theme.

The buyer's sale

One approach that doesn't require colour is a 'Buyer's sale'. With this, each department is given space and each buyer's photograph and name accompanies the final items at their final prices. The introductory copy reads:

> Each buyer illustrated is offering specially reduced prices on the featured merchandise. Each item is genuinely reduced due to overstocking—some are below cost and some even below half price. We have to dispose of these goods to make way for new stock.

The closing copy reads:

> These prices are genuine and we would like you to come in on Friday and Saturday to snap up these ridiculously low-priced bargains. We would also like you to come in next week and meet the new buyers.

A lighthearted finale to the sale.

Figure 8.1 is a unique example of a buyer's sale—a Pink Elephant Sale. The elephant in this instance was coloured pink, but although it is preferable to use colour, it isn't necessary, if your newspaper doesn't have a colour facility.

The introductory copy explains why the sale is being held and a humorous theme runs through the very readable copy. Although there are fewer items, the copy for each is well written:

> Go on! Surprise yourself!—Better still, surprise us! Buy one of our half price knitted suits (slightly shopsoiled still from falling off the back of a lorry).
> Emreco Twomax—eg. £39.95, now £19.95 They're a steal!
> PS. Please don't tell anyone where you got them.

Fig. 8.1   An unusual buyer's sale   When a store buys slow-moving merchandise it needs a special promotion to move it. This example is delightfully different. The original used pink on the elephant

This advertisement brought good results when the store's summer sale was several weeks old. It is an example of how to keep a sale fresh and alive.

Even at sale time, don't lose sight of the opportunity to sell the store in your advertisement. Use your regular style of logo and border; put in introductory copy and illustrations, even if it means restricting the number of items. Do not sacrifice the store's established image for the sake of moving marked-down merchandise.

The sixteen-hour sale

Itinerant traders visit towns and stage a one- or two-day sale from a hotel room or a church hall. Local traders are annoyed with the room hirer and the newspaper that carries the advertisement. Such traders generally pre-pay for their advertising and the copy withstands close scrutiny—however, if they turn out to be charlatans, their advertising is refused on future occasions.

What can a retailer do? If itinerant traders pose a real threat, stage an event occasionally to satisfy that type of demand. If, however, your position in the marketplace is above that type of trading, it is best to remain aloof.

For those retailers who do want to take a slice of this business, there are one or two tips on advertisement design that you can take from the experience of the itinerant trader. The first tip is to use the newspaper's own type in a line-after-line symmetrical layout that looks like a public announcement. The message needs to convey a sense of urgency supported by creditability. The urgency can come from the fact that the sale is limited—two days only, or better still, 16 hours only.

If the sale is to be held at the store, it is best isolated from normal trading by closing the day before the two sales days. If Sunday sales are tolerated in your area, then Saturday and Sunday are the two best days. However, most will want this event on a Friday and Saturday, so the closing day would be Thursday. The first advertisement on Wednesday tells the public that the store will close the following day while price tickets are altered.

If the event being staged is in an off-store location you won't need the closure day for isolation purposes, but you may need it to move the stock. Don't forget to tell people how to get to your sale;

draw a map if necessary. The second advertisement will only need minor alterations and the third one, which can be smaller, should say boldly that the event ends the following day.

In America, retailers are past having the warehouse clearance, they have extended to loading bay sales, parking lot sales or garage sales, where the merchandise is moved out of the store to the loading bay, car park or garage. One retailer in the States hires a marquee and has a tent sale. One can only assume that security and weather are not problems for such events.

Sales promotions without a sale

Unless it is a store's nature to live by low-priced merchandise and constantly appear to offer fresh bargains, promoting should reach out to the vast majority of the population whose first buying motive is the desire to have a quality home and lifestyle rather than to make a saving. Brand and quality play a major part in influencing the buying decision of these people.

The public has an insatiable appetite for home ideas; it is this demand that makes the Ideal Home Exhibition an annual winner and garden centres an attraction for many. People like time to browse and any store can capitalize on this interest by having its own exhibition.

One successful event that has been used by many retailers is a 'meet the makers' exhibition. In this promotion, the manufacturers not only help with the advertising costs—they also send experts to the store to offer advice. A well-known maker of hand-carved furniture actually placed a wood carver in the store on one occasion. On another, the radio and television traders of Edinburgh held an exhibition of hi-fi equipment in a local hotel and collectively secured the help of the major manufacturers.

This type of joint promotion has the benefits of selling a particular type of merchandise as against other consumer durables and services that make inroads into disposable income. The collective strength of several retailers brings greater support from the manufacturers. A good example is National Home Improvement Month, where every year the retail trade is supported by several manufacturers to make this event a huge success. Showcards, tickets, and window stickers are shared expenses and therefore cheaper. Greater cooperation from the newspapers is likely to be another beneficial side-effect. One section of the population that offers a lot of business are those about to set up home for the first time, and a growing number of exhibitions are being staged for the benefit of engaged couples. A special 'Brides' Week' would make a good promotion. In addition to newspaper advertising, the store could send engaged couples a mail shot. Other non-competing traders may find it to their benefit to join in with the store's promotion and share costs.

Certain calendar events give opportunities to promote. Every retailer sees the possibilities of Christmas with gifts and guests as the targets for promotion and to a lesser degree the same applies to Easter. But how many retailers use Mothers' Day or Fathers' Day as a platform to create store traffic? Only certain merchandise within the store may be suitable to feature in these special events—for example, in a furniture shop, Fathers' Day may be confined to desks and reclining chairs—but the object is to build store traffic.

Another similar event, not often thought of as an opportunity outside children's outfitting, is 'Back to School'. When starting school or moving to another school or college is uppermost in the minds of parents, an opportunity offers itself to sell a wide variety of goods, ranging from clothes to cycles, cameras, calculators, etc., etc.

The opportunities for promotions are limitless. Each department could have a departmental promotion. You can have a 'Charge it' promotion for your credit facilities, a 'Hostess' promotion for the start of the party season. Your major suppliers will probably support you with advertising for a 'Birthday' event, which incidentally doesn't have to be only for major anniversaries—you have a birthday every year.

Keep your customers

While the first job of an advertisement is to sell the merchandise featured, the longer-term function is to sell the store. Good advertising should find new customers and inform old ones, and, in an ideal situation, boost both the number of customers and the amount each one spends. Even in recessions there are some companies that manage to do this.

Advertising is the life-blood of mail-order companies and they do all they can to try to hang on to each new customer. Every buyer is a target for fresh offers made through the post. This is yet another leaf for the direct retailer to take from the mail trader's book.

Even someone who has purchased goods from you and been perfectly satisfied will not necessarily return to your store. Other retailers' advertising and store windows will be a counter-attraction for them.

Send your customers the occasional letter, tell them about your stock arrivals, or give them advance notice of your sales. Give them first refusal of any bargains that you may have to offer. There is a skill to writing sales letters and the whole business of selling by post, but the rules of copywriting still apply. Good sales letters still need to state the customer benefits and the reasons to buy at your store, to adopt the 'you' approach and to use ordinary language free of technical jargon. A badly-written letter without a clear proposition can do a store more harm than good.

Your customers—especially those with accounts—should be treated as a privileged group. Writing to them in that vein will add strength to the mail shot. If you refer to them in your mail-out as privileged customers, make sure that the offer you give them is exclusive. Your sale preview should be for your privileged customers, not for the general public. Except for the big single loss leaders, let them buy or layaway preferred items. You could have day or evening opening just for these customers. They should be the first to get invitations to fashion shows, demonstrations, beauty evenings, exhibitions, and other special events.

The proposition in your letter should be quickly and adroitly expressed, without surplus words, but with more than just a bare specification. There are several good books written on the subject of writing sales letters. The study of these will be repaid with extra sales.

Despatch books and accounts departments are the best source of names and addresses. Retailers who do not sell merchandise that needs delivering and whose trade is all cash can get the names and addresses of customers by other means. The most straightforward and least offensive way is to ask if the customer would like to be on the privileged customer list. An 'official' application form for privileged customer status and a counter card explaining that privileged customers will receive information about new ranges, demonstrations, special offers, and discounts will help.

The creative alliance

What makes a promotion work? The answer is storewide enthusiasm. A successful promotion is assured if all the staff are behind it. A creative alliance with staff on promotional matters is vital for two reasons. First, they have useful ideas for or about promotions, and second, they are the people who have to make a promotion work, and they will do so if they are committed. The misplaced enthusiasm of the boss who believes he is the only one who has the best ideas is detrimental to any creative alliance with the staff. Hold brainstorming sessions where the wildest ideas are put forward by everyone, and then utilize the best.

You won't want to label each week in the life of your business with a promotional title—ordinary business can be exciting too. Every week the trade press brings exciting reports of new lines, and that same sort of excitement should reach your prospects through your advertisements. One of the advantages of a newspaper is that you can pass on information at short notice when your new stock arrives. Be enthusiastic about your new stock, encourage your staff to be enthusiastic, and get the news into an advertisement while it's hot. Remember, it's possible to get sales long before you pay your supplier or your newspaper, provided that your credit is good.

Success factors

1. *There is no month when sales are too low to advertise.*
2. *Reflect the quality of the store*   Don't press the panic button in difficult times and have one cut-price event after another.
3. *Make sales credible*   Explain why the sale is taking place and why the prices are genuine.
4. *Start your sale on a weekday*   Give yourself an 'extra' big day's takings.
5. *Keep the sale fresh*   Don't use jaded phrases. Use the word 'tomorrow' in every advertisement and retain a sense of urgency every day of the sale.
6. *Sell the store*   Even at sale time, sell the store. Do not sacrifice

your image because it is sale time.

7. *Give ideas*   In-store exhibitions build store traffic because people want ideas.

8. *Get storewide enthusiasm*   Success comes from the enthusiastic participation of the entire staff. Hold brainstorming sessions to find the best ideas.

9. *New stock, new enthusiasm*   A new stock arrival is good news for your prospects so get it into advertisement while the news is hot.

Sell it fast and improve your cash flow

9.

Getting manufacturers' help

More and more manufactuers are prepared to help retailers sell their merchandise. The enlightened manufacturer no longer 'sells in', a euphemism for unloading wares regardless of whether the retailer will sell them or not. The manufacturer now sees the retailer as a 'sell through' outlet.

There are just about as many reasons for the manufacturer sharing promotional costs as there are for the retailer wanting to do so. Both retailer and manufacturer must share a concern about the slow growth in sales, the shrinking number of outlets, and the growth of multiples. The latter brings with it a growth in 'own labels', with subsequent erosion of some manufacturers' share of the market. It is common for manufacturers to express concern over the shift in power from brand to retailer. Most businesses want the widest base of customers that is economically possible, and manufacturers are no exception. Hence your store has a key role in your supplier's business.

Manufacturers benefit from helping their retail outlets with promotion costs—advertising where the merchandise is available increases sales, the outlet is encouraged to continue to exist viably for them, and their brand name is linked with a reliable, well-known retailer. A retailer hopes to derive much the same benefits from advertising, and the extra money from suppliers can be used to increase either the frequency or size of the advertisements.

The approach to procuring and controlling manufacturers' financial assistance needs to be systematic if it is to bring in the right type of support, with prompt settlement by the manufacturer.

The system is in six stages.

1. Decide who you want to share advertising and costs with. There

are many suppliers who will gladly offer support to get goods into a store, but it may not always be advisable to accept their help.

2. Find out upon what conditions the financial support is offered, and from this information calculate the amount of money due from that manufacturer.
3. Allocate the money consistently with the store's retail advertising plan.
4. Create the actual advertisements.
5. Display the goods that are advertised.
6. Collect in the manufacturer's contribution.

Depending upon the size of the store, this system requires key people to make sure the plan works.

Identify leading suppliers

Consult your purchase ledgers and list your top suppliers. In a small store there may be no more than 20, but a larger store may have 20 in each department. It is important to list only the *leading* suppliers—those whose products should already be featured in your advertising, and who produce the larger portion of your sales. These suppliers are most likely to heed your request for cost sharing, although there may be minor suppliers who would be delighted to advertise generously to enlarge their business with you.

Beware of the astute supplier who is happy to unload a heap of stock on the store and willing to pay the full cost of the advertisement, not just half. The cost of the advertisement is of minor importance compared with having the right goods to advertise. For this reason, if for no other, it is important to choose your advertising partners carefully.

Collect suppliers' information

Having chosen your manufacturers, write to them and ask how much they will contribute, upon what conditions and how settlement will be made.

The amount a supplier is prepared to contribute may depend upon your worth to them as an outlet. A well-organized supplier will have limits on the total amount payable (often a percentage of sales), while some offer a fixed sum to each outlet. Some manufacturers may offer 25, 75 or even 100 per cent of advertisement costs, but generally the retailer is expected to match the manufacturer's contribution pound for pound, and therefore they offer 50 per cent.

The organized supplier will want proof of insertion, in the form of a copy of the advertisement and invoice. The use of a standard block may be insisted upon, although an increasing number of manufacturers are prepared to let the retailer design the advertisement using the brand logo and, perhaps, a supplied illustration. If the conditions proposed are unacceptable, given your advertising and trading policies, then do not accept them, even if it means advertising the same merchandise at full cost to yourself. However, the majority of retailers find that, quite apart from the acceptability of the financial support, the offer of a free illustration, copy and brand logo is an additional benefit. Some of the best advertisements in local newspapers are the standard blocks that accompany shared cost space.

There may be a time limit on the offer of advertising support, particularly if the retail advertising is intended to coincide with a national campaign. To avoid problems on the day of financial reckoning, make sure the agreement is understood at the outset, and preferably confirmed in writing. Payment disputes often arise, but they are invariably the result of misunderstood agreements.

The best time to ask for advertising support is when the manufacturer's representative is taking an order. All buyers and managers should therefore be responsible for asking for manufacturer's support when buying, as part of their commitment to the creative alliance. At the conclusion of each purchase—or, better still, just before the conclusion—ask for advertising and promotional support and tie it in to your total sales plan. Ensure that whatever is agreed is confirmed and acknowledged in writing.

All buyers need to be conversant with the store's procedure for securing cooperative advertising funds. A standard form (Fig. 9.1) is useful for assembling the information from each supplier and on that basis you can calculate the amount of cooperative advertising you intend to build into your general advertising budget. This businesslike form is best filled in in front of the representative (a large firm would also need to keep a copy in the accounts section).

At the top of the form are the supplying company's name, the

calculate co-op money using a form like this

Co-operative advertising control sheet

Company _____   Sales representative _____

Product(s) _____
_____   Reimbursement
                                     requirements _____

Co-op terms _____
_____   Send to: _____

Accrual period _____   _____
_____   _____

Planned £ merchandise purchases	£ available for co-op	Date and size of ad	Co-op £ spent	Date invoice and tear sheets submitted	Date re-imbursement received	Balance of co-op £ available

Summary of planned allocation of co-op funds for year ending_____

JAN.	FEB.	MAR.	APR.	MAY	JUNE	JULY	AUG.	SEPT.	OCT.	NOV.	DEC.

NOTES:

Fig. 9.1   Use a standard form for collecting details of conditions that suppliers agree to pay towards the cost of advertising

representative's name, and the products they sell and those upon which they are prepared to offer an advertising subsidy. The 'co-op terms' refer to the percentage they will contribute and up to what ceiling, and there is space to set down the actual period of co-operation, the time limits of qualifying purchases, the reimbursement requirements (brand logo, copy etc.) and to whom the bill is to be sent. The columns below are a record of purchases, the co-op money due and spent, the date the manufacturer was invoiced, and the date the refund was made to the retailer. The use of a form also leaves your supplier in no doubt that you expect cooperative advertising and have an efficient system to deal with it.

Allocate the advertising money

A good retail advertiser will already have an advertising plan, with each department allocated advertising space for every month of the year. The goods to be promoted by cooperative advertising should feature in that plan when they are selling best. To do this, ascertain the peak selling time for those products and use the manufacturer's money to double the size of the advertisement or increase the number of insertions. The end result may be several manufacturers participating in one omnibus advertisement, or perhaps just one manufacturer and one retailer sharing one space.

The question of sharing an advertisement with other retailers often arises. If the alternative is several retailers taking out similar smaller advertisements, then it makes sense to cooperate. Competition does not only come from your particular classification of retail trade. The battle is for disposable income and the collective strength of a retail classification should never be underestimated. Nor should the combined strength of independents be underestimated when selling against the large multiple. This sort of promotion may be described as manufacturer-led, with the manufacturer matching the combined financial contribution from each retailer, and it offers the retailer less waste when the store's catchment area is smaller than the newspaper's that carries the advertisement.

Merchandise is what makes the character of the store, and advertising should reflect that character. The manufacturer-led advertisement illustrated in Fig. 9.2 is an example of an acceptable way for many retailers to share the cost of a larger advertisement.

Fig. 9.2 A shared-cost advertisement Sharing an advertisement with other retailers and a manufacturer lets everyone take full advantage of a wide newspaper circulation

Create the advertisements

Like any other advertising, cooperative advertising should above all else sell the merchandise. Second, it should promote the store's image and at the same time meet the requirements of the manufacturer, your partner in the promotion.

Many of the manufacturer's requirements also have benefits for the retailer. For example, the illustration is probably of a standard that reflects the quality of the merchandise. To take a photograph or make a drawing of similar quality could be a costly business. The manufacturer's copy is often not only well written but technically accurate, an important factor in the eyes of the Advertising Standards Authority. The brand logo may be famous, a sign of reliability that will inspire confidence and have a special significance to most intending buyers.

The words of an advertisement are its most important component. If in your expert sales opinion you feel that the selling message can be improved, or if you want to personalize the headline and the copy, you should do so, but only if you really can improve the advertisement's effectiveness.

An occasion may arise when you want to change or redesign the entire advertisement to improve its selling power or match your image. Alternatively, you may want to change it to include more manufacturers—this is more acceptable nowadays and only a few manufacturers insist on their products being featured exclusively with their own border. The effect is far more pleasant if the advertisement is simplified and organized so the eye can go freely from one item to another. It would be difficult for any manufacturer to criticize the effective advertisement in Fig. 9.3.

Merchandise the advertising

If the right goods are being advertised at the right time, the next logical step is to merchandise them. Every salesperson needs to know what you are advertising. They should be familiar with the special features and selling points of the products so that they are not at a loss when enquiries from interested customers begin. The windows and in-store display should also exhibit the goods that are featured in the advertisement.

The key to successful merchandising is advance planning, for all

Fig. 9.3   A retailer-led advertisement   Several manufacturers share the cost with one retailer in a well-organized advertisement

the good reasons explained in Chapters 1 and 2. Knowing what items are being featured means better briefing for sales staff and planning time for window and in-store displays. If you know what special promotions you intend to have before you even buy the merchandise, there is no reason why speculative visuals of the advertisement should not be drawn up to show manufacturers the quality and type of advertising and promotion they are supporting.

Just as the manufacturer was asked at the point of purchase for help with advertising and costs, he should be asked for showcards and display material. If your event is big enough, the manufacturer may have sales specialists or demonstrators to help you—you may never know if you don't ask. Your importance to your supplier is not governed by the size of your store, or even the size of your order. It is your personality, your potential and your enthusiasm that count.

If your copy is at the newspaper office on time for proofs, ask for extra copies. Some newspapers are also prepared to supply enlarged bromides for a charge that is modest related to the overall cost of the promotion. Your newspaper may also have 'As advertised' tickets and if not it is worth printing your own, so that you echo your newspaper message to passing prospects who may have seen the advertisement but need a reminder.

Some sophisticated retailers who plan their promotion activities well in advance not only present manufacturers with a visual of the advertisement they expect them to participate in, but also supply illustrated examples of the type of in-store display that will be given for their products.

Collect from suppliers

A good local newspaper will have a co-op coordinator and advertisement staff to advise you at every stage of your co-op action plan, and they will ensure that you have the necessary proof of insertion in the form of tearsheets, voucher copies, or invoices.

In most cases the newspaper invoices the retailer, and the retailer claims part payment from the manufacturer. This is often the most convenient method for both parties because the adjustment is made in the retailer's account with the supplier. However, the manufacturer or the retailer, or even both, may prefer to keep a separate account for advertising.

A few manufacturers place their retail support advertising in the hands of an advertising agency, but only a few because of the administration problems. The most effective schemes are through the company's area sales manager—a happy arrangement which gives the manufacturer a close rapport with outlets and the retailer good advertising and other back-up facilities.

Finally, it pays to monitor results from each advertisement, for your own and your supplier's information. It will facilitate future support if successful and allow you to adjust future programmes if not.

Success factors

1. *Choose your partners carefully*   Select only your top suppliers, the ones whose goods you sell most.
2. *Merchandise is more important than costs*   Even if you get no financial aid with advertising, the right merchandise is more important than the cost of the advertisement.
3. *Ask for cooperation when you buy*   The most crucial time to ask your suppliers for cooperative advertising is when you are ordering merchandise.
4. *Note any conditions*   Cooperative advertising is a two-way agreement—note and honour the manufacturer's requirements.
5. *Train all buyers*   It is important to brief them on maximizing and operating the scheme.
6. *Use a standard form*   To help avoid any confusion, use a control sheet for each supplier.
7. *Join forces for impact*   If your catchment area is smaller than that of the newspaper you use, big space impact can come from sharing with other retailers half the cost of the space.
8. *Promote at peak selling time*   When allocating the co-op money, build it into the overall advertising plan when the co-op items are selling best. Use the money to double the advertisement size or increase their frequency.
9. *Create the advertisements*   Build your advertisements using the elements from your manufacturer(s), making sure that they conform to good selling principles and at the same time reflect the image of your store.

10. *Merchandise* Make sure that the items advertised are displayed appealingly and sold well by the staff.
11. *Collect your money* Use your system to get the manufacturer's contribution—don't forget that copy invoices and tearsheets may be necessary.
12. *Monitor the results* After each advertisement, note sales; the information will help both you and your suppliers.

The good, the bad and the unorganized

To illustrate the previous chapters on advertisement quality and image, this chapter contains a selection of advertisements chosen for their good or bad points. It should be said that it is hard to find an advertisement that meets all the criteria laid down in Chapters 3, 4, 5 and 6. All too frequently advertisements are so unorganized that they cannot possibly reflect the efficiency of any store.

Some advertisements selected for their good points may also have many bad points, and vice versa. The intention is to expose some common faults and explode a few myths about good advertising.

Poor advertisements are often hotly defended with the cry 'But it brought results!' Any advertisement that brings satisfactory results should not be changed for the sake of changing—in fact it should be published again and again until the response peters out. Then it should be rested and tried out again at a later date or next year. But even if an advertisement did bring results, the next question must be 'Can it be improved, to bring even better results?'

Sometimes an advertisement may not look attractive but it gets response. This was certainly the case for a small tailor's business which for many years published an advertisement every February saying, IMPORTANT ANNOUNCEMENT at the top in the newspaper's own type. It was essential to use the newspaper's own type rather than a drawn heading to give it an air of urgent authority. It went on like this:

> In order to keep our workshops busy during this quiet period we are offering 10% DISCOUNT on all orders placed before the end of the month. Final fitting will be arranged at a time to suit you. It can be ordered now for autumn delivery.

This gave the story credibility and eased the prospect's buying decision; only part payment had to be made now and the rest could follow later, when the suit was complete. The tailor was well known to men, so the illustration chosen was a female in an elegant tailored suit. This was to emphasize that they also tailored women's suits. This one advertisement, only 20 centimetres by two columns, packed with information about materials and styles, turned a poor month into a very busy one for that tailor. It would never have won an award and it did not blazon the advertiser's name across the page but every single centimetre of that advertisement sold merchandise.

Improvements to many of the examples that follow would cost nothing extra. It must be worth checking if you too could get extra business with no extra cost by giving your advertisements maximum fire power. Some of the examples could end up costing less simply as a result of reducing the over-generous space that was bought to carry a tepid little message. Many, however, need either illustrations, good headlines or selling copy and in some cases all of these components to improve their effect. For these, extra space would yield disproportionately extra rewards.

It is easy to see with hindsight how an advertisement could have been improved. Producing a poor advertisement is forgiveable, once. Each advertisement should be a conscious effort to improve on the last.

Aim for the widest possible audience

'Mattress sales are around by the dozens these days. You can't open a paper or flip a dial without somebody's mattress sale shouting at you (eye and ear pollution).' This quote is from *Sek Says*, a book written by M. Seklemian of the Retail Reporting Bureau, New York. 'Sek', as he is know to all subscribers, has been in retail promotion for 50 years and he has very decided views about retailers who publish nothing but sale advertisements, especially those who do it badly.

The market for new beds is big in Great Britain, but the rate of new bed sales is not keeping up with what the demand should be. According to the Bedding Federation the gap is 15 million beds wide. People are buying or being given second-hand beds when for health and hygienic reasons they should buy new ones. People are managing on old beds that cause backache, Britain's number one illness. And yet, despite this, advertisement after advertisement appears aimed only at those people who are actually looking for a bed at that time.

The inducement usually offered is a discount. Some advertisements don't even carry illustrations, as well as having a weak or nonexistent sales story.

Enough has been written about illustrated advertisements (see Chapter 5), so I shall not repeat that message here. In any case, many bedding advertisers are well supplied with illustrations from manufacturers.

'Big B' (see Fig. 10.1) is a typical bedding specialist taking a typical bed advertisement which conveys the impression that a good range is to be found at the store. This advertisement may well have been the best bedding advertisement in that particular newspaper, and as a result a large proportion of those people in the market for a bed that day may have responded. But what about the other 15 million who really need a new bed? They kept their money in the building society or used it to buy a video or a foreign holiday.

The Aberdeen Bedding Centre advertisement (Fig. 10.2) has the same failing. Their approach is to try for impact; the advertisement aims to make a small space, and in particular the name, jump out of the page. The graphics of this advertisement are good, the illustration is dominant, the name is dominant, and they link from top to bottom. The problem is the selling message, which is too brief and tucked in wherever it will fit. The only selling point mentioned is the price which is presumably reasonable.

This advertiser could have produced a better advertisement by using a manufacturer's standard block and getting assistance towards the cost. Many retailers argue that they should not pay 50 per cent towards the cost of an advertisement when they are getting 20 per cent or less of the space for their name and address. In this instance it would be preferable to have a headline that promised a benefit rather than an oversized name.

What do manufacturers say in their advertisements about beds and mattresses? Slumberland, for their Ivory Seal bed, list the product points as: deep stitch quilted, jacquard damask mattress cover;

Fig. 10.1   A typical well-stocked bed specialist advertisement should get a good response from those people who want a new bed

Fig. 10.2 An advertisement with good graphics, but not an ideal selling advertisement

layered new cotton felt over natural fibre upholstery; timber framed 11″-deep solid top divan; posture springing in the mattress—unique to Slumberland—and they list the sizes. Comfort, the prime benefit of beds, is sold in the following manner:

> Posture Springing is the only mattress springing system that's actually designed for sleeping on—and it's unique to Slumberland. In practical terms, it means an even, comfortable support that adjusts itself to the weight placed on it. And because all the springs are linked together they mould themselves to the body contours for a more natural sleeping position.
>
> No sagging, more comfort and more restful sleep—that's what Posture Springing means to you.

That is the type of copy, with selling points and benefits that extend the reach of the advertisement beyond the immediate

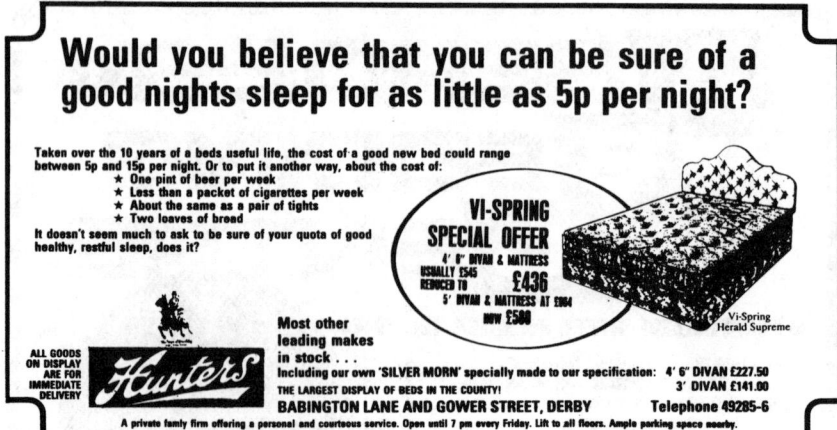

Fig. 10.3 A thought-provoking headline is a good start, but the advertisement needs selling copy on the importance of restful sleep

price-conscious few who at present sleep on broken beds, or settees, or on the floor.

When first-time buyers are fewer, it pays to go for the replacement market, the affluent middle-aged who are drinking less, saving more, and whose children are away from home so they are free to go abroad more often. These are the people who can afford to listen to the finer points about quality and comfort.

Hunter's advertisement, Fig. 10.3, is nearly there. It uses a thought-provoking question for its headline, but even so it does not follow through by selling the quality of the beds well enough, or the importance of good deep sleep. The headline would have been better left with the question 'How much should you pay for a good night's sleep?', followed by a smaller subhead 'You'll pay less tomorrow with this special 20 per cent saving.' A golden rule is to talk cost at the end of the sales pitch, even in this novel advertisement with its unique cost comparison.

One of the advantages a specialist retailer has over a department store is that of being able to claim to be the consumer's advocate. The fact that a store specializes is a unique selling point. Some retailers choose to demonstrate their specialization subtly by implication, like 'Big B'; some like to punch it home, like the Aberdeen Bedding Centre; and some like to make an issue of it, like

Fig. 10.4 Emphasizing the USP This advertisement is a specialist's advertisement even without the cartoon at the top which is used to emphasize Kleinsleep's unique selling proposition compared with a large department store

Kleinsleep (Fig. 10.4) which stresses the unique selling point of immediate delivery.

All merchandise needs selling and, although these three examples feature beds, the same mistakes are made in all categories of retail advertising and the same principles of headline selection and copywriting are applicable whatever the merchandise.

To sell properly you need room. Very often it takes only a little extra space to convert a shouting advertisement into a powerful, persuasive sales story. The extra space can often be found by the reduction of name size, (as could easily have been done in Fig. 10.2), a reduction in the size of illustration, or by dropping one or two items.

Dare to be different

Many advertisers believe that being different is the prime objective of an advertisement, which of course is not true. The prime objective is to sell, and the second objective is to pre-sell the store as a nice place to shop. Somewhere among the objectives of an advertisement you can add the suggestion that 'it was a nice place to have shopped'. All those customers who have used the store over the years should still feel a glow of satisfaction whenever they see an advertisement, knowing that the store's good qualities remain. Even though most advertisements from established companies get more than half of their response from past customers, very few customers are so loyal that they can't be tempted elsewhere, especially if new stores—competitors—are opening to lure them away.

The continuous chain of sales may bring instant response but when, through this barrage of bargain advertising, does the store's true image have a chance to shine? Many stores have so many sales that they are like itinerant traders who have stopped roving and settled in one town.

In Fig. 10.5 David Morgan dares to be different with this advertisement, not in an ugly way, but very simply, by putting the largest logo at the top of the advertisement upside down and using it in an imaginative headline. How much more memorable this sale advertisement is than one that says 'Ends tomorrow'. The figure in the advertisement is an action figure. It captures movement, it is dominant, and it is placed diagonally opposite to the

Fig. 10.5   The main namestyle is turned upside down and this simple action makes a memorable difference to the advertisement

traditional position of illustrations in advertisements.

The use of the name at the top, in the middle, and at the bottom of this advertisement is acceptable in this case. It is used *in* the headline, not instead of the headline, and it is used where readers expect to find it, at the bottom. For good measure, it is also cleverly used in the middle of the artwork. All tall advertisements should use the logo three times to keep the name near the offers. Note too the way the £ symbol in front of the prices has been dropped, improving the neat and tidy look.

No advertisement is totally perfect, and even in Fig. 10.5 one or two more words could have been added to improve the description of each item, to give extra sell at no extra cost. Where it really scores is on individuality, which far too many retail advertisements lack. It is a good illustration of how an advertisement can dare to be different.

Simplify and organize

Advertisements featuring more than one department need good organization to help the prospect find the items they want. Simplified advertisement layouts are the most effective. When a store has just two departments and each appear to be divorced from the other, like the example of footwear and floor coverings in Fig. 10.6, it could be argued that the best way to overcome the problem is to publish separate advertising for each department. In reality, this store has obviously found itself a unique niche in the marketplace. Given that it may be better to combine two unusual departments in one large advertisement, composing this requires special care. It requires, for example, one good umbrella headline and a good sub-head for each department.

If the words 'A square deal for everyone at Winfield's' are not a slogan, they should be the basis for the headline—if they are they should be smaller and part of the name block. 'A square deal for you and your family at Winfield's' would make an umbrella headline ('You and your family' is more pertinent than saying 'Everyone').

Illustrations should contribute to the sales energy of the advertisement. They should be dominant and relevant to the sales message. Are those boots and shoes the ones featured in the copy? Why

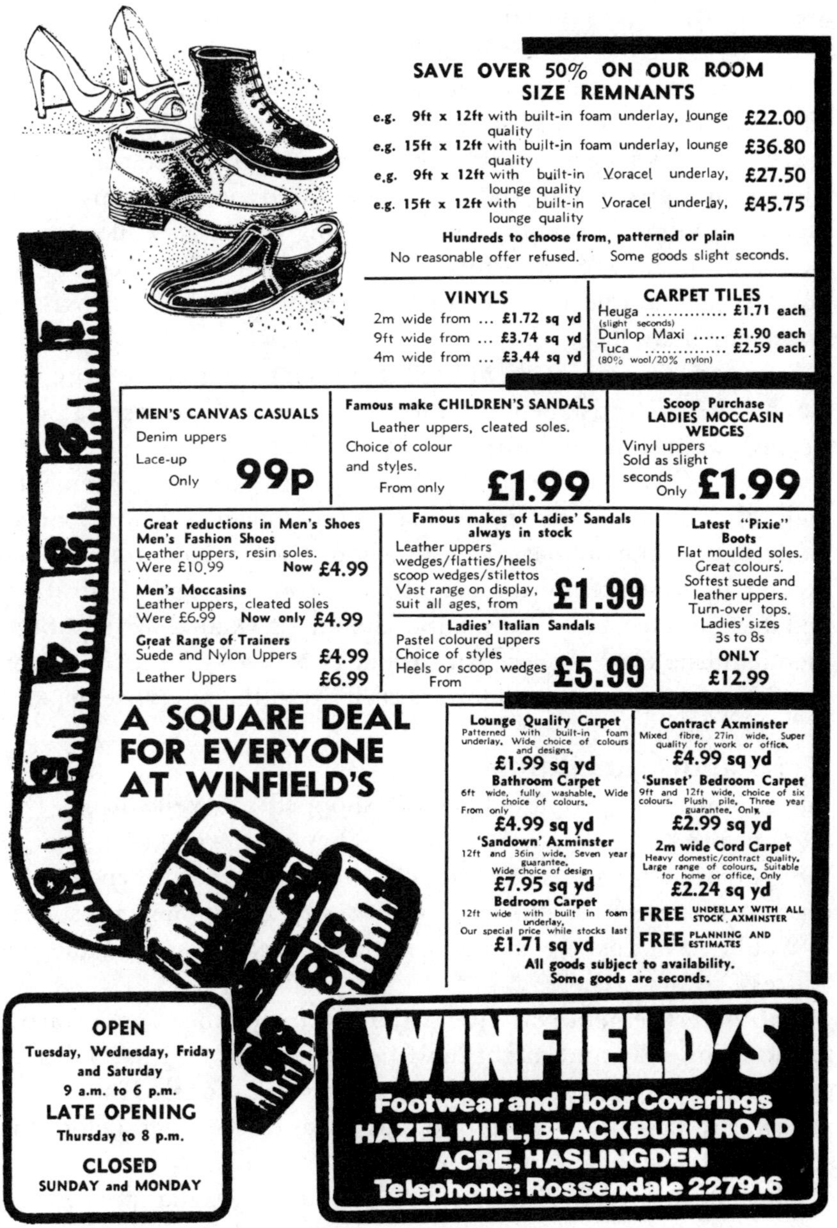

SAVE OVER 50% ON OUR ROOM SIZE REMNANTS

e.g.	9ft x 12ft with built-in foam underlay, lounge quality	£22.00
e.g.	15ft x 12ft with built-in foam underlay, lounge quality	£36.80
e.g.	9ft x 12ft with built-in Voracel underlay, lounge quality	£27.50
e.g.	15ft x 12ft with built-in Voracel underlay, lounge quality	£45.75

Hundreds to choose from, patterned or plain
No reasonable offer refused.   Some goods slight seconds.

VINYLS

2m wide from ... **£1.72 sq yd**
9ft wide from ... **£3.74 sq yd**
4m wide from ... **£3.44 sq yd**

CARPET TILES

Heuga .... **£1.71 each**
(slight seconds)
Dunlop Maxi ...... **£1.90 each**
Tuca .... **£2.59 each**
(80% wool/20% nylon)

MEN'S CANVAS CASUALS

Denim uppers
Lace-up
Only **99p**

Famous make CHILDREN'S SANDALS

Leather uppers, cleated soles.
Choice of colour
and styles.
From only **£1.99**

Scoop Purchase LADIES MOCCASIN WEDGES

Vinyl uppers
Sold as slight
seconds
Only **£1.99**

Great reductions in Men's Shoes

Men's Fashion Shoes
Leather uppers, resin soles.
Were £10.99   Now **£4.99**

Men's Moccasins
Leather uppers, cleated soles
Were £6.99   Now only **£4.99**

Great Range of Trainers
Suede and Nylon Uppers   **£4.99**
Leather Uppers   **£6.99**

Famous makes of Ladies' Sandals always in stock

Leather uppers
wedges/flatties/heels
scoop wedges/stilettos
Vast range on display,
suit all ages, from **£1.99**

Ladies' Italian Sandals
Pastel coloured uppers
Choice of styles
Heels or scoop wedges
From **£5.99**

Latest "Pixie" Boots

Flat moulded soles.
Great colours.
Softest suede and
leather uppers.
Turn-over tops.
Ladies' sizes
3s to 8s
ONLY
£12.99

A SQUARE DEAL FOR EVERYONE AT WINFIELD'S

Lounge Quality Carpet
Patterned with built-in foam underlay. Wide choice of colours and designs.
£1.99 sq yd

Bathroom Carpet
6ft wide, fully washable, Wide choice of colours.
From only **£4.99 sq yd**

'Sandown' Axminster
12ft and 36in wide. Seven year guarantee.
Wide choice of design
£7.95 sq yd

Bedroom Carpet
12ft wide with built in foam underlay.
Our special price while stocks last
£1.71 sq yd

Contract Axminster
Mixed fibre, 27in wide, Super quality for work or office.
£4.99 sq yd

'Sunset' Bedroom Carpet
9ft and 12ft wide, choice of six colours. Plush pile, Three year guarantee. Only.
£2.99 sq yd

2m wide Cord Carpet
Heavy domestic/contract quality. Large range of colours. Suitable for home or office. Only
£2.24 sq yd

FREE UNDERLAY WITH ALL STOCK. AXMINSTER
FREE PLANNING AND ESTIMATES

All goods subject to availability.
Some goods are seconds.

OPEN

Tuesday, Wednesday, Friday
and Saturday
9 a.m. to 6 p.m.

LATE OPENING
Thursday to 8 p.m.

CLOSED
SUNDAY and MONDAY

WINFIELD'S

Footwear and Floor Coverings
HAZEL MILL, BLACKBURN ROAD
ACRE, HASLINGDEN
Telephone: Rossendale 227916

Fig. 10.6 Headline and subheads needed   This advertisement needs simplifying and organizing

are they adjacent to the copy on floor coverings? What mystic motif is the tape measure? If it is an identification motif, it should be made smaller and the valuable space saved could be used to insert an illustration—in this case probably carpets. More valuable space is lost through untidy typesetting. Prices and items float in white space, space that could have been used for more copy to sell each item more thoroughly. Neater setting would also allow space for the headline and subheads. The panel containing the hours of business has ample room to include credit facilities and parking arrangements.

Every advertisement should reflect the character of the store and maybe the advertisement in Fig. 10.6 does; it suggests a well-stocked, old-fashioned, untidy business.

A well-stocked store needs to have well-stocked advertisements, and this advertisement is no exception, but two items (one of footwear and one of floor covering) should be singled out and given greater prominence by the use of more copy, a good illustration, and a large price. Every advertiser should get excited by the store's merchandise, even if there isn't room to write and illustrate each one fully. Great values call for enthusiasm in the advertisement.

Merchandise at all times

Presumably, the people who have shopped at Wellworths (Fig. 10.7) before know where the store is. They may even know some of the type of merchandise that is sold, but no advertisement should miss, as this one does, the opportunity of recruiting new prospects. It would have cost no more to put in merchandise and the full address.

The advertisement was intended to be an advance notice for the forthcoming sale, and might have been intended by the retailer to offset a competitor's sale which started a week sooner. If so, it was misconceived. Who will shop at this store in the week before the start of the sale, before prices have been reduced?

There is no week in the life of any retail business that presents no opportunity to sell. This advertisement should have carried one or two top-selling lines, even if it meant pulling forward those lines from the sale. Bargains on sale now are a far better way of counter-acting opposition than an advance announcement that is likely to

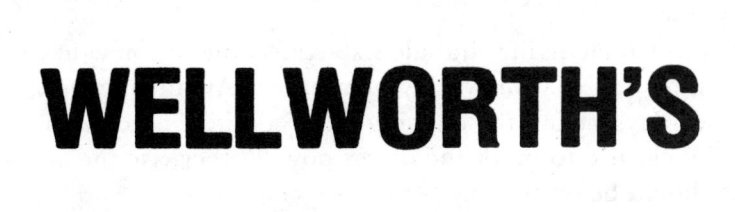

WELLWORTH'S

SALE

—— COMMENCES ——

**WEDNESDAY
29th APRIL**

★ FULL DETAILS IN NEXT WEEK'S PAPER ★

Fig. 10.7   An advance sale announcement   Should a retailer publish one?

do more harm to your sales than to your competitor's.

One Sheffield store discovered that a rival was starting its summer sale a week sooner than they were. In an attempt to offset this, they staged a special towel offer. They offered top-quality towels from America, whose retail prices were higher than normal British towels. In one week the store sold a greater value of towels than in a full year. The towels, together with other special purchases, gave a better-than-average week's takings without pulling the sale forward in a panic.

It is worth changing the sale's starting time to coincide with the publishing day of your weekly newspaper. An advance notice of a sale two days before the opening is a good idea if you announce a one-day closure to mark the prices down; otherwise the advertisement should be on the day before the sale starts.

If an advertisement can be read in 15 or even 30 seconds, ask yourself if the message might not reach more prospects via commercial radio for the same money. (But remember that with printed media you have the advantage of being able to use illustrations and long copy.) For more on radio advertising see Chapter 11.

Test and adjust

Advertising has always been part of the operational plan of Caines of Newport but, like most independent retailers, they have always been subject to budget limitations. In better times an advertisement like Fig. 10.8 brought results despite its disordered layout, its awkward squat shape, and its shortage of selling copy. G-Plan is a well-known brand and Caines boasted large stocks. Six photographs endorsed the big stockist claim, even if they were not clear pictures. Past research shows that preference for branded merchandise is three and a half times greater than for unknown brands.

David Caines changed his advertising after attending a one-day seminar held by B.A.S.I.C. He utilized the Bedell principles and developed a style that brought results even in the depths of a recession. Attaining an ideal standard of advertising was a case of test and adjust. The main changes were in the copy. Instead of mere labels or stock lists, the copy was full, informative, and persuasive. Sometimes the copy was so effective that customers came in with the advertisement in their hands.

David Caines begins writing his advertisements with a list of questions to which prospects might want the answers. Some advertisements simply comprise the questions (in black type) followed by the answers. Sometimes the questions are anticipated, as in Fig. 10.9. A furniture buyer wants to know 'Will it fit?' The mini-illustrations and sizes from the Stag brochure provide the answer. This was one of those advertisements that prospective customers

Fig. 10.8 One of Caines' 'before' advertisements It was effective because of Caines' size, G-Plan's popularity, and the message multiplication factor of the media

brought with them to the store. Caines now creates selling copy that appeals to both the head and the heart. Each advertisement sells the dream, the pride of ownership, while at the same time offering the reality of good value with all its necessary reassurance. In Fig. 10.9 the copy reads:

> Begin your day by waking up to a beautiful bedroom.
> Enjoy the warmth of Minstrel's rich cherry mahogany finish which blends most effectively with many different decor styles. Whether your scheme is traditional, country charm or sophisticated, Minstrel is one of the outstanding choices of the 80s. Most important, it will still be fashionable in the year 2000.

This opening enlarges upon the headline story. It sells the dream, it reassures the prospect that it will harmonize, and finishes by implying that the purchase will be an investment. The next section, with its own subhead, invites participation:

> The master bedroom needs special planning to be both functional and glamorous. The size of the bed, amount of chests needed. These are the starting points. Plan it out from our chart with a careful look at all the measurements.

The copy continues making use of the fact that Caines is a family firm:

> When you call our helpful sales staff will suggest many variations and decor. Discover the difference when you deal with a family firm. We'll give you the service you expect and deserve.

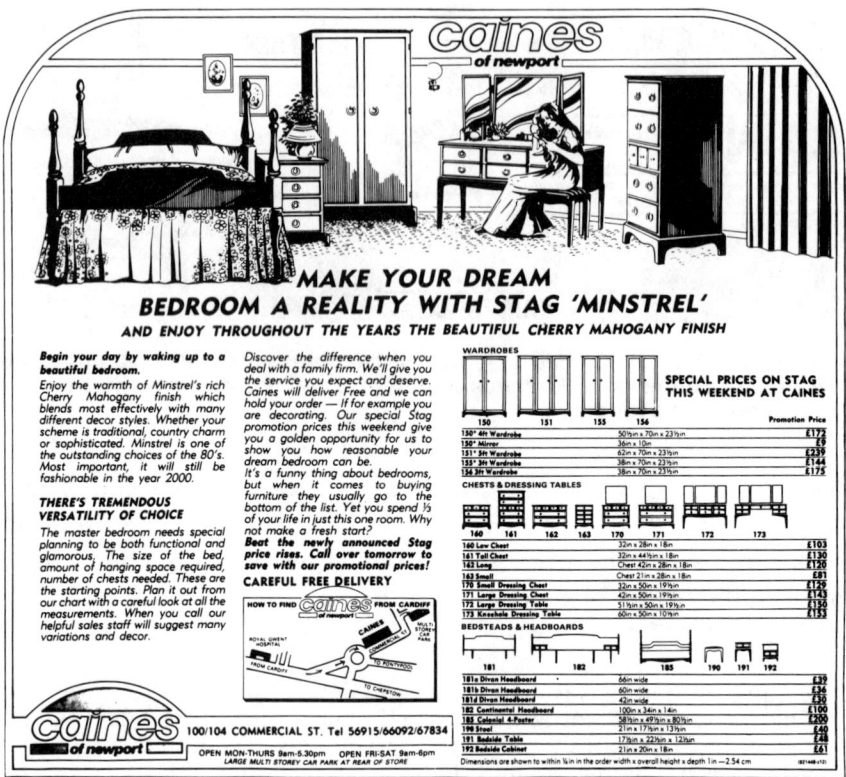

Fig. 10.9   One of Caines' 'after' advertisements   It was effective even in recession because of its useful information content

Even possible resistances or objections have been thought of:

Caines will deliver free and we can hold your order—if, for example, you are decorating.

The prospect then might be thinking 'I'll buy when I'm ready', but the copy goes on to dispel that notion with a reason for buying now:

Our special Stag prices this weekend give you a golden opportunity for us to show you how reasonable your dream bedroom can be.

Bedroom furniture is a low priority for its share of disposable income and even this is countered, and at this stage one can almost hear the Welsh accent because it is colloquial:

It's a funny thing about bedrooms, but when it comes to buying furniture they usually go to the bottom of the list. Yet you spend one third of your life in just this one room. Why not make a fresh start?

Finally, finish with a sense of urgency. Here, without any loss of dignity, the advertisement repeats the promotional price offer but adds a rational extra inducement:

Beat the newly announced Stag price rises. Call over tomorrow to save with our promotional prices!

It is one thing to use advertising to move regular merchandise, but it is an entirely different game to buy in optional or venture stock outside the traditional sale periods. Figure 10.10 shows that this can be done, however. The advertisement sold an entire delivery of leather chairs.

The selling copy uses much the same formulae. It gives emotional and practical reasons for buying, with a great deal of conviction. Sometimes low prices need to be justified if the reader is not to assume that the merchandise is inferior. This is how Caines combined the family business angle with an advantageous price:

David Caines has talked Ekornes of Norway into a once-only scoop release of a limited number of these chairs and stools in a fashionable and popular shade of brown leather. So at the price of an average fireside chair you can now enjoy the incomparable qualities of leather . . . its looks, its feel and even its beautiful smell. What else looks better as it gets older—becomes gracefully mature rather than soiled or worn out.

Quite apart from the persuasive copy, this advertisement has a dominant illustration of the product with a smaller squared illustration of the chair in use. It has headline and subheadings, full address, a distinctive namestyle, a map and it is all framed in a specially designed border.

The advertisements are bigger, the headlines longer, and the selling copy fuller, but they are organized to sell through picture, headline and subheads and to get their proposition across quickly and clearly. The detailed copy is there for those who require the extra information before visiting the store.

Fig. 10.10   A special 'venture' stock promotion   This advertisement sold the entire delivery of leather reclining chairs

Success factors

1. *Repeat good advertisements*   No advertisement should be changed for the sake of change. A good advertisement should be repeated as often as the market will stand it.

2. *Sales are the best guide*   A good advertisement is not one that wins an award but one that brings results. Every advertisement taken should be an improvement on the last.

3. *Use a selling idea*   Headline the best selling idea for the mer-

chandise to appeal to the widest possible audience of real prospectus.

4. *Support benefits* By using the specifications of the product, support each benefit with selling points. Make the most of unique features, as Slumberland does with its posture springing.

5. *Enlarge upon the headlines* Having aroused interest with the headline, make sure that the copy quickly follows with full details.

6. *Show your specialism* If you are a specialist shop, make every advertisement exude your specialism. You should be the consumer's advocate. Show it by the range and type of stock advertised and services mentioned.

7. *Advertise for tomorrow's takings* A week's advance notice of a sale can cost you valuable sales in the interim. Only advertise merchandise that can be bought tomorrow.

8. *Say 'save' when you say 'sale'* Every sale advertisement should mention specific items, even if only a few prime examples, and the words 'save' or 'saving' are equally important in the headline.

9. *Be different* Make your advertising different from other stores', but keep it in tune with the unique character of your store.

10. *Keep typesetting neat* Untidy type suggests an untidy store. Keep it neat and it is easy to read.

11. *Avoid wide typesetting* Copy much more than two columns wide (8 centimetres) is difficult to read.

12. *Keep the elements in logical sequence* The headline goes at the top, name and address at the bottom, and the copy in departments with illustrations adjacent to the relevant items.

13. *Full copy for key items* Some items—at least one from each department—should have full copy treatment, conveying value with a reason for buying. Answer all possible objections and include all the vital facts in simple language.

14. *Use subheadings* Each individual department needs a subheading above the copy. Big blocks of copy need to be broken up with subheads at relevant points.

15. *Make it easy to read* Do not use small type or white-on-black type—both make it difficult to read.

16. *Communicate fully* Newspaper advertising is more than just 'getting your name before the public'. If the message can be

read in less than 15 seconds, perhaps it should be on commercial radio or a poster.

17. *Pictures alone won't sell* Even when the manufacturer is sharing the cost and providing the merchandise illustrations, good copy is still vital.

18. *Make your offer unique* Try to tie the offer you are making to your store alone. You don't have to be a sole stockist to do this.

19. *Make the proposition clear* Don't let your anxiety to fill the space, particularly if it is large or an unusual shape, trap you into confused thinking. Keep sight of the logical sequence of ideas, and don't let the advertisement turn into a mass of headlines.

20. *Shape is important* A narrow strip across a page suits only a few advertisers (generally those who have a short, simple message). Keep advertisements taller than they are wide if the size is below half a page. Occasionally, however, the artwork may dictate otherwise.

21. *Keep your name near the offers* On big advertisements, use the store name more than once within the advertisement. Place the logo at the top, in the middle, and at the bottom.

22. *Use simple layout* Don't let the design of the advertisement conceal the message or even part of it.

11.

Radio 'Theatre of the Mind'

By the mid 'eighties, when 69 independent local radio stations are expected to be operational, about 90 per cent of the population of Great Britain should be able to listen to independent local radio. It is possible to broadcast a simple message to a large audience relatively cheaply, often to parts of the retail catchment area that other media cannot reach.

Differences from press advertising

No book on retail advertising would be complete without some advice on the use of local radio. Some of the principles that apply to newspaper advertising also apply to radio advertising, but there are important differences. Radio has some advantages over newspapers and newspapers have some over radio.

The most significant disadvantage for the retailer is that radio advertising lacks the flexibility that one needs for a full advertising plan, as described in Chapter 2. It simply is not feasible to feature several items from every department at least every month. On the other hand, it is possible to cover a full year's advertising plan by broadcasting several different messages each month, and the cost of production needn't break the bank. Costs will vary according to the size of the station and the station's charges for producing the cassette. Small retailers get better value if their premises are located within the broadcast area of a small radio station, because they are buying less waste.

The rules of good copywriting (see Chapter 4) are equally pertinent to radio advertising, but they need some adaptation. A well-written newspaper advertisement is unlikely to work used word-for-word on radio—for one thing, it will probably be too long. You can't use an illustration in a radio commercial, and you can't even use big type. This makes it vital to follow all the principles of good headlining. You must catch the listener's attention with words. Opening statements must intrigue, must talk news or promise benefits, always in conversational language.

Someone reading an advertisement is likely to give it full attention, but the ear is less attentive. To overcome this it is necessary to repeat key facts. Statements on radio need to be kept simple and brief. The listener does not have the advantage of instant replay, as the reader does, who can re-read the advertisement until the message is fully understood. In a newspaper advertisement, you can use your logotype as your identity tag, and it can be quite small because if the advertisement has sold well, readers will read the smallest type to find out where you are. With radio this is not possible, so to compensate you must repeat your name at least once, making sure it is associated with the offer. The listener must believe that the offer is uniquely yours and not available elsewhere.

To make up for the lack of illustrations, the copy should paint a word picture. It has to achieve this despite the fact that there are generally fewer words in a radio commercial and that many words have to be repeated. Phrases must be to the point, and selling points and benefits carefully selected for their persuasive appeal. Painting a word picture is not as difficult as it may sound, because the listeners use their own ideas to fill any gaps. For example, if the radio message says 'She's a beautiful girl', each listener supplies a mental picture that fits his or her own ideal. It could be argued that colours come across better on radio, because listeners picture the exact shade of colour they like best.

While it is desirable to read the copy for a printed advertisement out loud before finalizing it, it is essential that you do this for broadcast advertisements, and preferably get a colleague to listen. Some words or phrases that look right in print sound far from right when spoken. On the other hand, the inflection of the voice can change a statement's entire meaning, allowing you to achieve more in fewer words.

Numbers are important

Figures are a weak link in all advertising. They are the most frequent source of costly printing errors, because typesetters cannot absorb numbers as they can words. The same applies to radio listeners, yet some advertisers give lots of prices, a telephone number, and in some cases even an extension, in the hope that these will be remembered. It is best to use only one price and one telephone number in a 30-second spot, but to repeat them two or three times, making sure each time that they are very distinct.

With radio it is advantageous to use third-party phraseology—to say, for example, 'At Smith's tomorrow' or 'You'll love Smith's new cosmetics counter'. This is more difficult to carry off with conviction in a printed advertisement, set in a border, in your style, with your logotype (often at the top); there can be no doubt who is really speaking. If, however, you are using an announcer and not a store spokesman, the store should be referred to by name, not as 'we'. This is an advantage because it gives your business a quasi third-party endorsement.

You can get away with a poor headline in a newspaper advertisement if the rest of the advertisement is effective. With radio you don't get a second chance. If your lead-in does not attract the right prospect's attention, the rest of the message will fall on deaf ears. The nature of broadcast advertising demands repetition if the maximum audience is to be reached and the fullest advantage of the production costs taken. Therefore, the lead-in needs to be effective to avoid waste.

The principal differences between newspaper and radio advertisements suggest how to get the best possible results from radio advertising. Balancing all the disadvantages are equal advantages open to the copywriter who thinks carefully about getting the message across.

Writing a radio advertisement

In a 30-second advertisement you can get in approximately 75 words of normal commercial language. It's common sense to avoid long words and complicated language. The substance of the message needs to be carefully selected because of the limit on words and the need to repeat salient facts. The listeners need to know who is making the proposition, what the proposition is, why they should take advantage of it, and how and when they can do so.

A lot of radio advertising is used for special occasions—sales, bargain events, special weeks, etc.—where, because the story is simple and the number of items featured small, 30-second spots are effective. For example, the opening of a sale needs only one item and a lot of excitement in the advertisement, like this:

> Starts tomorrow! Scott's summer sale! See racks full of good buys . . . hundreds of offers. Prices cut left, right and centre . . . big, big savings wherever you look. For example, a manufacturer's clearance of ladies' shoes at half price. Sets of luggage that were £42 . . . tomorrow, only £32.99 at Scott's. For men, shirts at half price. Just a few of the many, many wonderful bargains waiting for you. Save tomorrow . . . in Scott's sale. Be there at 9 a.m. sharp for the best bargains!

An advertisement like this is designed to sell a sale throughout the store, although it can't list lots of merchandise or even one item from each department. It would be effective in its own right but would work even better if used to support newspaper advertising, in which case it could say 'See tonight's *Gazette* for many, many more bargains', in place of 'Just a few of the many, many wonderful bargains waiting for you.'

Immediacy is important. This advertisement says 'tomorrow' twice and invites people to get to the store at 9 a.m. sharp. No advertisement in any medium that says 'For two weeks', or even 'For two weeks only' is going to have much impact. Prospects will still be intending to come to the sale even after it's finished.

Notice how the name is used at the beginning, in the middle, and at the end of the 30-second announcement above. If it was a 45-second spot, the name should be used at least once more, and at least twice more for 60 seconds. (If you are making a 60-second advertisement, it should be written in two 30-second halves even if you do not intend to use it split up. This is a good test for identity and effectiveness.)

Three of the store's best-selling lines are used to demonstrate the value to be found in the sale. It is important to select only the best-selling lines that are carried in depth, for the same reasons given in Chapter 4. Where radio advertising is concerned this applies with greater force because of limitations on the number of words used.

Tempo

There are several reasons why advertisements written to be read differ from those written to be heard. One important factor is tempo. A radio advertisement must be able to cut through the preoccupations of the listener, whatever he or she is currently doing. The pitch and the speed of delivery are important—a slow voice invariably sounds unenthusiastic but, on the other hand, you need to avoid the insistent, unrelenting over-excited, strident tones that so many announcers use for commercials. The radio commercial should be written in speakable segments rather than in sentences. Very few conversations are spoken in sentences. There should be brief pauses, at least long enough to allow the announcer to breathe. The pauses should be at strategic points where the announcer can also change the pitch of his voice.

Selling a single item rather than an event requires many of the techniques of direct selling. Inside 30, 45 or even 60 seconds, the product has to be sold in a one-way sales conversation. A monologue can be avoided by using two speakers, one of them to ask and the other to answer questions about the product (see page 116).

Let's go back to the example of Scott's and their sets of luggage at the former selling price of £42. Thousands of people are going to have the opportunity to hear the advertisement, but out of these thousands, you have to select the prospects, make sure they listen, and persuade them of the major benefits. The lead-in should hit the right prospect immediately—in this instance, the word 'travel' is sufficient to capture their attention. At £42, price is still the biggest benefit and should be quoted early in the announcement. This is how one might make a 45-second commercial:

> All the luggage you need to travel the world for just £42. Where? . . . Scott's of course, the store that's known for reliability . . . A robust four-piece, matching set of three cases and a flight shoulder bag . . . Scott's checked them for reliability and value and decided they were the best you could buy for less than £50. . . . Each case has polished metal fittings, double buckle fastening, safety straps, all-round centre straps, and all the features you would expect from reliable luggage at a much higher price than Scott's price of only £42 . . . Scott's, the High Street, Nutwood, first for reliability and good value.

This copy sells both the store and the luggage. It uses the principal benefits of price and reliability. The rush of selling points sounds a lot in a radio advertisement, but many have been omitted (materials, linings, locks, label pockets, choice of colours) that could have been used to support the quality arguments in a press advertisement. The last words of the advertisement are not the address, but a selling sign-off line to give the advertisement a touch of personality.

Occasionally, merchandise may require more words than can be used in a radio campaign, because of the variety of items for sale or the nature of the product. In this case, you can only support your press advertising with an advertisement that sells the store's benefits. Start by finding the biggest reason why people should shop at your store. If you are a specialist retailer, it will probably be your speciality. If you have several branches, it may be convenience. If you have many departments, it could be your one-stop shopping convenience, and so on.

There are advantages in using lots of short spots. It makes the copywriter cut out generalities, forces the copywriter to be specific, and demands top-selling lines. It disciplines the writer to keep the message within a given time limit at an understandable tempo.

Two voices

One technique in radio advertising is to use two voices. Used correctly, this can more than double the value of the advertisement. The effect can be to put the listener in the position of an eavesdropper—all part of what broadcast exponents call the 'theatre of the mind', with the listener participating in the charade, hearing a two-voice question-and-answer session to some of the questions he or she may have asked.

A two-voice commercial is better accommodated in a longer advertisement; in fact a 60-second spot can be monotonous with a single voice, and memorable with two voices. It also gives the advertiser the opportunity to develop two characters for a series or an entire campaign.

You will notice, if you listen to radio advertisements, (which you should before going ahead with your own), that the best two-voice commercials are those that contrast the personalities of the two actors. It is possible to stretch the limits of humour a little further in a broadcast advertisement without damaging the image of the business—by pitching, for example, a bold character against a timid one, or a 'know it all' against a 'doubting Thomas'.

Only rarely is an amateur's voice suitable for radio, yet many advertisers cannot resist recording their own advertisement. The result can be embarrassing. There are exceptions—for example, when an actual customer is giving a spoken testimonial or a retailer is making a pledge. Both these occasions benefit from the sincerity with which the message comes across when spoken by the actual people concerned.

Jingles and music

There is a distinct and important difference between jingles and music. Music can endorse the character of the store just as much as the typestyle of a printed advertisement can. Jingles are entirely different. They may be good for a single product, like a chocolate-covered fudge bar, or a service, like British Airways. They have one message, lots of times to repeat it, and the budget to do it. If a listener doesn't catch the words the first time, then there are other opportunities. Jingles can obscure the message, robbing the retailer of the asset of direct speech.

Local radio stations hold music stock books with all types of music to match the character of your business. Some even have jingle backgrounds, for topping and tailing your announcement— this not only makes the advertisement distinctive, but separates it from others and adds continuity to a radio campaign.

There is a considerable cash benefit to using stock music, because it saves recording and royalty charges. Stock music is exclusive to your business and is generally offered free of charge to the advertiser or included by the radio station in a set production charge which includes the recorded voice. These stock cassettes come in two lengths, a 60-second base and a 30-second base.

Radio stations also have standard brand bases. Like the music, they come from America, so only when the brand is international and the voice suitable can they be used in Britain. Saving on production costs is not the prime objective: the first objective is to sell the merchandise and the second to sell the store. These objectives should not be pushed aside for the sake of using a free base.

Preserve the right image

One advantage offered by most radio stations is the ability to broadcast an advertisement at short notice—in some cases, within the hour, depending upon other bookings. While advertisements produced at short notice can be hot news, it is conceivable that the problems could outweigh the benefits. Even in the most urgent case, it is better to be a little late, but right. A retail advertisement relies very much on clear enunciation and on being in character with the store. The image of your store is just as important in the broadcast medium as it is in print, and yet in the former it is more easily misrepresented because of the theatrical nature of the medium. A fast-talking excited voice is fine for the bargain store; the up-market store should use a slower (but not boring) voice that uses pauses effectively. Pauses are radio's equivalent to white space. Retailers may not be professional writers but have unbeatable knowledge of their own stores and merchandise, so it is not only cheaper but better if they write their own scripts.

Radio advertising has one big advantage for the retailer with an unusual name: it provides an opportunity to get the correct pronunciation over to the public. Before radio, the best course of action for retailers called Cockburn was to change their name.

Synergism

Many campaigns start with a 60-second announcement that is followed up by shorter spots. To economize, advertisers may split the 60-second advertisement into 30-, 15- or event 10-second spots. Because the smaller spots are subdivisions of the parent advertisement, they echo the theme and aim to achieve synergism (the effect where, although the listener is listening to the shorter fragment, they hear the longer version, or, in the case of television voice-overs that are based on radio, they hear the radio but see the picture).

Success factors

1. *Intrigue your listeners* Make your opening statement capture attention.
2. *Repeat key facts* Repetition of key facts will improve listeners' retention.
3. *Repeat your name* Use your name at least twice every 30 seconds.
4. *Make your offer unique* The listener should feel that the mer-

chandise you are advertising is available from your store only.

5. *Paint a word picture* Use the principal selling points and benefits to paint a word picture of your offer to compensate for the lack of a picture.

6. *Repeat numbers* Listeners have difficulty remembering numbers, so use them sparingly and repeat them often.

7. *Use third party* Write your advertisement as if another person were talking about your store.

8. *Read your advertisement out loud* Test your phraseology for a smooth flow.

9. *Use simple words* Use everyday language that is clearly understood, and avoid long words if possible.

10. *Combine radio with newspapers* If you have a lot of sale items, put them in a newspaper advertisement and use radio to draw attention to your newspaper advertisement.

11. *Create urgency* Say 'Tomorrow', not 'For two weeks only'. Make the listeners believe that if they are not there tomorrow, they will be unlucky.

12. *Best sellers only* You don't have time for lots of items, so pick only the best sellers.

13. *Get the tempo right* A slow voice can sound unenthusiastic, a fast one gabbled. Use a modulated voice, with pauses and an occasional change of pitch.

14. *Sell the store* If it is a product that is being advertised, sell the store as well. If products can't be featured, sell the store anyway.

15. *Two voices double the effectiveness* By contrasting one voice against another, you can intrigue your listener more effectively.

16. *Use customer's voice for testimonial* A satisfied customer saying why your shop is best adds credibility to your message.

17. *Music portrays store character* Use music that matches the character of your store in advertisements, for identification purposes, but beware of jingles that can obscure the message.

12.

Merchandise is the magnet

The High Street is the shopper's Mecca, and with or without advertising most stores there flourish. Large British retailers occupy the main street of the towns and cities, so shoppers find the same names in every High Street of every town.

These same retailers will only move into new shopping centres if the centre is a sound proposition. Part of the soundness of that proposition comes from the other tenants of the centre. A good example of an out-of-town shopping centre is Brent Cross on the London North Circular Road. This purpose-built centre has two well-known department stores (John Lewis and Fenwicks), plus the other well-known retailing names (Boots, Marks and Spencer, Burtons, W.H. Smith, C & A, Dixons, etc.).

The appeal of the High Street

Plainly, the retailers are the High Street, a factor more important than the geographical location of the street itself. The High Street's allure comes from a combination of shopping area size—large enough to buy all one's requirements on one shopping expedition—and the concentration of so many retailers in one area. If this concentration of retail premises is diluted by the encroachment of building societies, banks and offices, the allure fades and the crowds dwindle.

Convenience is also part of the allure—the ability for shoppers to reach the street by whatever means of transport is at their disposal. In the case of the out-of-town shopping centre, the attraction is the size and convenience of the car parks. The allure is also people—the busy crowds whose presence confirms that going there to shop is right. It is the reputation of the stores who trade there—big, well-known, dependable names. It is the price range—shops and stores to cater for all classes of shoppers at the price to suit them. The allure is community indentification. The High Street relates to the community it serves, over many years it has ascertained the needs of those who shop there.

One attraction, however, stands out above all the others: merchandise. Here in the High Street the shopper feels he or she will find the lastest fashions, the best value, the widest selection, the lowest price, the greatest expertise, the latest innovations, or the perfect gift. The merchandise is the magnet. The finest service, the most wonderful displays and the brightest lights will be to no avail if the merchandise is not right.

The allure of the High Street is a formidable problem for the smaller retailer who occupies a different location. Since the end of the Second World War, the independent retailer has been losing the battle to the multiple trader. It hasn't been a bloody battle, for many retailers have sold their businesses or their leases for sums of money that make the struggle nugatory.

Combined advertising

If your problem is one of location, it is particularly important to plan so that every single centimetre of advertising you buy works to its fullest extent. Your battle will be easier if your retailing neighbours are of a similar disposition and prepared to bid for business. By joining forces with other retailers in your community, whether you are in a suburban shopping centre, a street, a village or a dormitory town, you can make your shops an Aladdin's cave, an oasis of interesting goods at fair prices.

Regular advertising by every retailer working to an individual plan will benefit the district, especially if the advertisements are grouped together within the newspaper. Many newspapers can be persuaded, or may even be anxious, to put community advertisements into an advertisement feature. While the offer of a free editorial write-up is attractive, the end result may not bring in the desired sales for the participating retailers. The editorial may be sterile, the advertisements dull and uninspiring, and if each advertisement is within its own distracting border, the whole page may simply be skippped by the reader. Here are some ways you can lessen the risk of this happening.

Promote a theme

Promoting a shopping district is similar to promoting a store: it is best done to a theme or around an event. If you are already holding meetings of traders for other purposes, such as rates, parking restrictions or other domestic matters, you have the platform already established to propose the event or programme of events. If not, the biggest step is to get your fellow retailers together and devise your promotional theme. The name of the promotion is less important than the effort that goes into it.

The freer the discussion, the more likely the meeting is to find the right theme, but the theme will be only as good as the extent to which the retailers develop and exploit it. If the meeting turns into a healthy, brainstorming session, jot the ideas down for future promotions. It is important not to allow any good idea to slip away.

One peripheral but important advantage of this meeting—and indeed for any individual who decides to advertise—is that it constitutes a subconscious step towards ensuring that the advertisement lives up to its promise. This should apply to a street, a shopping centre or a village just as much as it would to a store. Be proud of your retail community.

Features

A dull 'Shop in our street' feature won't do much good; the aim should be to create a promotional event.

In features, most newspapers offer a fixed quota of editorial in relation to advertising, which can vary from 10 to 50 per cent, but the newspaper controls the content of the editorial. It is desirable to find out before the meeting whether the newspaper is prepared to allow the equivalent amount of space so that, instead of a feature, you could have a promotional composite advertisement. Your newspaper editor may prefer this arrangement because few local newspapers have a commercial feature writer and the editorial in a district feature tends inevitably to be viewed as something just to keep the advertisements apart.

If a composite with a free space allowance is not acceptable to your newspaper, it's worth paying a professional press relations writer to write the editorial of your choice. If the editor will not accept this either, consider paying the full cost of the space yourselves. It is more important to say exactly the right things in your promotion than it is to get free space.

Features must be labelled 'advertisement feature' and composites must be labelled 'advertisement' clearly at the top. It is important to have a clear understanding with the newspaper on which category your promotion falls into. If it is indistinguishable from a newspaper feature but you have controlled the wording, then it must be labelled 'Advertisement'. The Code of Advertising Practice says: 'An advertisement should always be so designed and presented that anyone who looks at it can see that it is an advertisement without having to study it closely'.

The next stage is to list the benefits from the shopper's point of view of shopping in your area. These benefits will probably be similar to those of the High Street, even if they are scaled down a little. How close is your community to being described as a one-stop shopping centre? You may never have realized all your area has to offer until you get around to setting down a full list of the possibilities in the form of an advertisement. Suburban shopping localities are especially convenient for those who live locally and, while the appeal may not extend to the entire catchment area of the newspaper, it probably reaches well beyond the area's immediate surroundings. Suburban shopping areas are cosy as well as convenient; individual ownership fosters customer care and attention, and community identification is often of a very personal nature. These benefits to the local shoppers want stating.

Create extra benefits

In addition to the ongoing attractions of the shopping centre, there will be the benefits and excitement that the promotion has created—discounts, free gifts, fun, personality visits, competitions or whatever extras have been decided upon.

One novel idea from an American downtown association was a mystery discount promotion. The retailers in Downtown Fargo gave a mystery discount card to each purchaser. The card had a scratch-off cover over a number between 10 and 40, entitling the purchaser to a discount between 10 and 40 per cent. The average was 12½ per cent and there was a maximum value to the goods that qualified for the discount.

An idea used by the Scotmid Co-operative Society in Edinburgh, and one that would lend itself very readily to a neighbourhood shopping unit, was a 'Good Neighbour Month'. Shoppers were invited to nominate a 'Good Neighbour'—someone, maybe, who unselfishly helps senior citizens or the disabled with their shopping or gardening, or helps organize events for young people. It can be anyone who is doing good in the community without seeking reward. A prize in shopping vouchers was awarded for the best nomination. This is a good way to gain community recognition and, although such an event is advertised, an editor could hardly fail to cover in the news columns the very human stories that are bound to come to light.

The Butts Shopping Centre in Reading runs regular promotions with strong themes. Probably the best is 'Children's Week', which is designed to alleviate mothers' problems during school holidays. A programme of events for children involved the Early Learning Centre, the Children's Library, a travelling theatre and a TV star. It is a popular public-spirited promotion that attracts customers and is good PR at the same time. The same centre also runs a 'Butts in Bloom' promotion when the public are invited to bring in their pot plants and flowers for a competition. It's a good idea for a covered shopping centre, a town version of a village show.

The shopping malls of America are the most advanced in their promotional activities, with all manner of events to entice the public: children's theatre at school holiday time, entertainers on the fourth of July, back-to-school coupons in the early autumn, photographic and art exhibitions, and even, in the case of La Cumbre Plaza in Santa Barbara, a real wedding to which the public were invited. This pace set by the new shopping centres and out-of-town shopping has stimulated retaliatory action by the old town centres commonly known as 'downtown' in America.

It is important that the promotion should not rely on advertising alone; other ingredients are necessary. Prize money may have to be found, and some suppliers may be prepared to help. It's certainly worth asking them. The event has to make an impact and point-of-sale material for windows and displays will be necessary.

Always bear in mind that the theme is only the packaging, and don't make the mistake many shopping centres do of advertising the theme alone. The heart of the venture has to be the merchandise.

Dig out the right merchandise

The success of any promotion is not measured by the quality of the event, nor the beneficial effect on the community, nor the publicity it creates, nor the coverage in the press. It is not even measured by the crowds it draws. The only true measure of success is the amount of sales a promotion produces. Any boost to goodwill or community identity is peripheral and to be looked on as a bonus.

If sales are the measure of success, the merchandise has got to be right. Each participating retailer is charged with the responsibility of digging out the right merchandise at the right price, even if this means producing loss leaders for their advertisements. In this case the retailer is like a store buyer, responsible for finding merchandise that is news because of either its price or its uniquiness, and for expressing its qualities in an advertisement.

The objective is to produce a page full of ideas and thereby convey the impression that your shopping centre is full of bright shopping opportunities. Make the page flow. Try to avoid borders that separate various retailers' advertisements—a top and bottom rule are all that is necessary. Use a benefit-promising headline at the top of each advertisement and keep the name and address in proportion to the rest of the space each retailer is taking. It is important for each retail outlet to take a space according to its anticipated sales, so individual advertisement sizes will vary.

A theme is only a catalyst. Advertisements should still observe the same golden rules as they would if they were individually placed in a run-of-paper position. Make sure that you and your fellow retailers agree on these rules for there should be no fruitless panels in the composite. Don't allow any participating retailer to take space simply to support the promotion, even if the free space increases because it is in ratio to the paid-for space. Top to bottom, side to side, the composite should be full of wanted, desirable merchandise.

Every advertisement should also devote space and words to sell the general benefits of the store, shop or trade. Each advertiser should make the customer feel wanted and at ease.

Manufacturers' support is important in this type of venture. If you share the costs, you can achieve the largest possible advertisement, and, even more important, the manufacturers' brand names inspire shoppers with confidence. Your suppliers may give additional help on special occasions, with the loan of demonstrators, showcards, display, sale or return, for example, as well as support with advertisement costs.

Get a visual prepared

You may need professional help in laying out a composite advertisement because this could be larger than any individual retailer has taken in the past. The newspaper should provide a satisfactory layout service after the theme has been decided and rough details drawn up as a brief for the artist to prepare your visual from.

All goods advertised should be displayed and prominently ticketed. The prospect has the right to find the merchandise advertised, and manufacturers who support you have the right to know that you are actively selling their brand.

Link up with other retailers of similar goods

Another form of association promotion that deserves consideration is a joint promotion with members of the same trade. When several retailers belong to a trade association or sell a similar product or service throughout the circulation area of one newspaper, it makes sound economic sense to share an advertisement.

The collective strength of a network of small retailers is a powerful counteraction to one large town-centre retailer from the same trade. Wholesaler-led buying groups use this strength to some degree with the favourable buying terms they can procure, but little has been done to produce a combined selling strength. There have been modest attempts by Nu-mark, the chemists' buying group, and various grocery groups, but they do not match the firepower of big advertisers like Boots and Tesco.

A three-way contribution to the advertising programme is called for—one third from the manufacturers, one third from the retailer and one third from the wholesaler—to provide sufficient funds to run a competitive campaign.

Profitable coverage

An association promotion that is spread over a newspaper's entire circulation area makes use of the maximum number of copies sold, because most readers will have a stockist near them. This is just the opposite to a district feature, which has to ignore the fact that much of a newspaper's circulation may be wasted. For a suburban retailer, circulation on the other side of town is of little use unless what the store has to sell is so unique or such an incredible bargain that prospects will travel long distances to buy.

A growing number of newspapers are prepared to editionize their circulation so that suburban retailers can buy a section of the circulation more localized for their purposes. Weekly and free newspapers tend to be more parochial in their circulation and you buy less waste with their more compact coverage.

There are advantages to using a larger daily or weekly newspaper, of course. One of these is the 'presenter effect' of the medium; your advertisement may be in the more prestigious medium directly opposing the advertising of the town centre stores. This is poor compensation for excessive waste, however.

Before any promoter is reconciled to having to buy circulation that is of little use, the following steps are worth taking.

1. Get a quote from a printer for printing the composite in newspaper format.
2. Get a quote from a reliable distributor for distributing the composite to every door within the catchment area.
3. Find the number of households that take the local newspaper.
4. Compare the cost per household covered by the newspaper and the distribution method.

Alternatively, see if the newspaper is prepared to weight up its paid-for coverage with a distribution of pre-prints of the promotion.

Your own feature

On the opening of a new business, an anniversary, or an extension, it is possible to get suppliers and contractors to take advertising

Fig. 12.1 Two pages from an unusual eight-page supplement Instead of writing about Davies Wallpapers, this supplement is a useful eight-tabloid-pages guide to decorating

within a retailer's own feature. The bigger the retailer's parent advertisement, and the more support advertising that is obtained, the greater the amount of editorial the newspaper will give and the more pages the feature will run to. It's a golden opportunity to get a lot of 'free' publicity—so much publicity, in fact, that there is the danger it may not be matched with sales. What often results is an editorial that interests the retailer and family more than the prospective customers. This self-indulgent editorial is backed up with advertisements that congratulate the retailer upon his or her achievement. All this happens in the one issue of the newspaper. It would be far more beneficial if the publicity were spread over several issues or even weeks. An editorial history of the business is only of limited interest to readers and, on the principle that they are more interested in themselves than in you, the editorial is best used to offer the readers help and promise benefits.

The advertisement for Davies Wallpapers in Fig. 12.1 is a good example of this. The retailer has devoted the editorial space of an eight-page tabloid-size supplement to a reader's guide to interior decorating, a much better way to be recognized as an expert than writing about the store. The only improvement to this supplement would have been to reduce the heading on the inside pages from 7 centimetres by 6 columns to 4 centimetres by 3 columns and use the 180 centimetres that were saved to illustrate the text matter on other pages. A further tip for those who do buy two full pages across the centre of any publication: see if the gutter between the pages can be used. In this instance Davies wasted a further 39 column centimetres—enough to itemize a decorator's accessories for example.

Congratulatory support advertisements from suppliers and contractors should be selling advertisements. Suppliers should feature the best-selling lines that the retailer has in stock.

The contractors' advertisements should say (with a photograph, if possible) what their part was in the contract and they should also invite other work by selling the contractor's service. If there is an interesting story to tell about the retailer and the premises, let it lie alongside the contractors' advertisements and let the manufacturers' advertisements form a composite around a strong sales message for the store.

The key to successful joint promotions, whether a community composite, an association composite or a retailer-led promotion, is to make every single column centimetre sell.

If your local newspaper invites you to participate in a feature, only do so if its audience is clearly defined and the subject matter interesting. Do not rely on the feature heading and editorial to do the selling. Make your advertisement sell independently from the feature.

Success factors

1. *Devise a theme* Hold a meeting with your neighbouring retailers and decide on a theme for your joint promotion.
2. *List the benefits* Decide and list the benefits your shopping locality has to offer prospective shoppers.
3. *Fulfil the promise* If you make a collective promise, be sure each retailer lives up to it.
4. *Control the 'editorial'* It is more important to say the right things than to get free space. If you can't have control of all the space in the promotion, pay for it, so that you can.
5. *Create extra benefits* In addition to the integral benefits of your area, create extra ones for the promotion.
6. *Identify your promotion with the community* Try to give your promotion a public-spirited angle.
7. *Seek suppliers' help* If the participating retailers get their principal suppliers to share costs, the advertising will be greater. The suppliers may also offer promotional help.
8. *Merchandise must be right* All participating retailers should promote best sellers—interesting merchandise.
9. *Give the page continuity* Don't let each retailer's advertisement be boxed in by a border. Treat the page like a store advertisement.
10. *Make the group dominant* Keep each participant's advertisement subordinate to the theme. Don't let any retail store's name outweigh the merchandise in its space.
11. *Do a value-for-money check* Does the promotion in the newspaper offer better value in cost per household reached than a leaflet drop?
12. *Make 'editorials' interest the reader* Readers are more interested

in their own comforts and needs than your history.

13. *Make every advertisement sell*   Every advertisement from every participating retailer, supplier, or contractor should sell.

14. *A page full of interest and ideas*   Readers will remember your retailing locality as full of interest and ideas if your page is like that.

13.

Inside information

The advertising and marketing glossographists cloak their activities in techniques and terms that suggest advertising is an accomplishment best left to experts. In fact, there is no mystery either to creating advertising that sells or to the mechanics of getting it into a newspaper or on the air. This chapter is written to explain the less obvious benefits that can be obtained from the media and some of the details that agencies do or should concern themselves with on behalf of their clients.

Classified advertising

One of the advantages of the competitive world is that any would-be business can start advertising for a few pounds. No matter how small or new your business is, it is possible to buy something and sell it at a profit by using a classified advertisement, even if it is just two lines.

Classified advertisements are found grouped together on pages that contain nothing but advertising, and each advertisement comes under some group heading. This grouping and classifying attracts prospective buyers; they will look for the classified section and read the columns that cater for their special interests. Here prospects are looking for advertising, whereas with display advertising in newspapers, advertising is looking for prospects.

There is no need in an individual advertisement to attract the attention of a prospect—he or she will already have decided to read the columns that are of interest. It is advisable to begin the advertisement with the product for sale and follow with the principal benefit, which in the case of classified advertising is mostly (but not always) price.

Because most classified prospects are looking for a particular item or service, long advertisements are best avoided. A better strategy is to separate the advertisement into single items or groups of related items to make the copy, which will inevitably be in small print, more digestible. It works out slightly more expensive this way because of the number of part lines that are being paid for as full lines. To compensate, however, all or parts of the advertisement are more likely to be read.

Most newspapers offer the opportunity of placing display advertisements in classified columns and also, at a more favourable rate, semi-display advertising. Semi-display advertising is a style that offers varying sizes of type and white space within the column. No illustrations and only one type is usually allowed. Both display and semi-display are bought by the single column centimetre and they are a neat solution to the trade advertiser's problem of requiring longer copy than a private person is inclined to use. All trade classified advertisements must clearly indicate that they are trade.

Classified advertising is one way of advertising in every issue of a daily newspaper to achieve a form of continuity. It is ideal for the services that a retailer offers but often overlooks, such as repairs, making up, installations, or perhaps the store restaurant.

There are people whose interest in a newspaper goes little or no further than the classified columns. To put before these people the full range of merchandise that you have in your run-of-paper advertisement, you could use the appropriate columns with lineage advertisements or even small semi-display to draw attention to your main advertisement.

Classified advertising is a good, if somewhat cautious, way to sell merchandise while at the same time relating advertising expenditure to expected sales. For some retailers in the larger cities where the ROP display advertising rates in city newspapers are high, it is the only form of advertising they can afford.

Colour

You may have the chance to use colour in your advertising, given the spread of web offset printing facilities among newspapers. The use of a single colour, known as spot colour, can be worth the extra investment but it can also be a waste, and sometimes it can even detract from the sales message of an advertisement. Colour should be used for extra impact, for the clearer classification of departments, for selling colour or for atmosphere.

For impact it should be used in big bold masses of eye-catching colour—red, blue, green, but preferably not yellow. It is not sufficient to take a black-and-white advertisement and substitute colour for some of the black. All colour advertisements should be designed for colour. There are lots of permutations when one adds a colour. Just as there is black on white and white on black, there is now the opportunity to have colour on white and white on colour. It is possible also to have black on colour and a colour on black, although there may be technical problems with these extra configurations.

The actual impression on the paper in web offset is made by a roller blanket which transfers the images from the colour and the black and white printing plates to the paper. The problem is that the black can transfer back to the colour printing plate and thereby contaminate the coloured ink. Amongst other factors that affect this are the quantity and colour of the ink used. Yellow, apart from its disappointing appearance on newsprint, is easily contaminated. A lot of black and a little colour can also be a problem, if your advertisement calls for a small dash of colour out of a black mass. If you want to be ambitious, consult the production manager or a qualified adviser from your newspaper.

Colour may also be used for classification, to relieve the monotony of an item-packed advertisement by breaking the material up into readable segments. To do this, you use colour for frames and reversed subheadings. It is not a good idea to print the copy itself in colour: small coloured type is difficult to read, and 18 point (¼-inch) type should be the smallest size you should consider for printing in colour.

Colour to sell colour is an interesting concept but it requires the full cooperation of the newspaper printing department to get the exact shade of colour you require. It may be a new fashion colour that is being featured, a new shade for a motor car, or the colour of a label. Whatever the reason, the newspaper must be able to offer accurate register and an exact colour match.

There is growing interest in full colour, known as process colour, made achievable in newspapers by the web offset system. Even so, throughout the country the newspapers able to offer the facility are still in a minority.

Process colour is expensive because in addition to black, a separate printing plate is required for each of the three primary colours, and each colour picture used needs a separate negative for each colour. The cost quoted by the newspaper usually includes one set of colour separations for one picture; subsequent separations for other pictures cost extra.

Large multiple retail advertisers do not normally use process colour because it is not available in all the newspapers they are likely to use. For smaller retailers colour is expensive, but the majority of those that have used it have done so on a shared-cost basis with a manufacturer who has also been able to supply excellent colour photographs, or even separations.

Colour for atmosphere is an underused technique, probably because the artwork tends to be more complicated and therefore more expensive than it is for the more simple uses of colour. The possibilities for creating atmosphere by the use of colour are numerous—blue skies for holidays, an orange setting sun for a Mediterranean evening, green fields and hedgerows for a rural housing development. Colours reflect moods: marine blue for coolness, an orange glow for warmth, purple for richness.

Overall, colour improves the pulling power of most newspaper advertisements, particularly if your advertisement has the exclusive use of colour on the page.

Coupons

Mail-order traders use coupons in their larger advertisements for high-priced merchandise to reduce mistakes in orders. The public does not expect or even feel inclined to fill in a coupon to a retailer's advertisement when they can go and see the goods in the store.

Coupons, when used correctly, allow you to test either the product or the advertisement. The only way effectively to test an advertisement is to have two different advertisements for the same merchandise in one day's issue, if the newspaper is able to carry them. A split run, which is the technical name for this, can only be done by a newspaper office that uses a double unit press. The copies that come from the left-hand side of the press have one advertisement and the copies that come from the right have alternative copy. Both advertisements carry coupons that are redeemable against the purchase of a particular product. This method ensures that the advertisments are evenly distributed on the same day over the newspaper's entire circulation area. Newspapers that offer this service charge extra for it to cover the cost of setting and a second plate.

The most effective use of coupons is made by manufacturers, particularly food processors, producing low-cost products that are universally available so that the coupons can be redeemed anywhere.

There is a credibility gap when coupons are used for big-ticket items, especially if the advertisement says something as general as 'This coupon is worth 10 per cent off all purchases'. If you wish to use coupons, be specific. Name the item and state a cash value for the coupon, as in the advertisement below:

> A special offer to all mothers who read the *Gazette*. This coupon entitles you to £2 off a school blazer—cut it out and bring it along with your child for a fitting tomorrow while stocks last. Only available to readers of the *Gazette*.

A couponed advertisement needs to abide by all the rules of good retail advertising. The coupon needs to be purse- or wallet-sized (no bigger than a banknote) and it should not occupy more than a quarter of the entire advertisement. The rest of the space should be selling the benefits of the product and reassuring the reader that you will welcome the coupon. Give a reason why you are making the offer—any good reason, not just a desire to test the medium.

The newspaper should be instructed to place the advertisement on the outside edge of the page, preferably at the bottom corner of the advertisement. If it is in the right-hand bottom corner then the advertisement should be placed on the right-hand side of a right-hand page at the bottom. This makes it easy for prospects to cut the coupon out.

Campaigns

Advertising to a plan could be regarded as a continuous campaign, but the word 'campaign' has a special significance to the professional marketeer. A campaign is a series of advertisements linked by a common theme or reason. The annual sale advertising is inevitably a campaign; the event links the advertisements and most retailers use the same sale block throughout the sale period.

A campaign has a familiar recurring note to it through the artwork, headlines or copy, but preferably through all three. The danger with campaigns is that they can be boring. Brilliant copy is to no avail if people don't read the advertisements. Each advertisement should be sufficiently different to get itself read. To this end, each advertisement should have its individual selling headline as well as the campaign theme. An overline or campaign logo should be a separate piece of artwork across a corner or beside the company name. Some part of the advertisement's body matter should also relate to the campaign theme—ideally each advertisement should have copy that follows the theme right through.

No matter how clever your idea, how beautifully drawn your overline. or how unique your copy, the success of a campaign ultimately depends on how desirable your merchandise is.

Christmas is probably the time of year that best lends itself to a long-running campaign. You can start as early as you feel decent and run right up to a last-minute gift suggestions advertisement two days before Christmas. The advantages are obvious, the continuity this period offers when most retail sales are peaking allows a retailer to build a Christmas store image.

The Christmas theme logo cannot be too specific if all departments are going to share the same umbrella for 10 weeks or more. It's got to be general: 'It's a Dickens of a Christmas at . . .', 'Jones' the Christmas Store', 'The most treasured gifts come from . . .', or simply 'Joy, Joy, Joy'. Because Christmas is a long shopping period it would split into two campaigns, the first in November with the theme 'Shop for Christmas in November—Relax in December'.

The other necessary ingredients are a Christmas border, a bauble or two, and copy that is written with Christmas in mind about merchandise that is wanted at that time of the year. Branded lines can be tied in with a famous-name campaign. A theme like 'Famous names you'll find at Jones' this Christmas' could be a powerful persuader for getting manufacturers' assistance with the costs.

The main objective of a campaign is to ensure that full benefit is derived for both sales and the store's image from the cumulative effect of advertising.

Typestyles

No one expects a retailer to be an expert on type, the newspaper printer least of all. Type mark-ups—the trade terminology for specifying what size type the headlines, subheads and body copy are to be set in—can cause big problems when an amateur tries to do them. Some newspapers do not publish a book of their typestyles because of these problems, but you ought to know the range of typefaces available.

You need to lay down certain rules about the types to be used in your advertising. First there is size; sizes from 5 to 72 point are widely available and some newspapers can supply type even larger. Type sizes are quoted in points, 72 points being approximately one inch. Five or even six point type is very small and should not be used. For headings and subheadings ideally you should not use less than 14 point.

The two most popular typestyles are Roman and Sanserif. They are popular because they are both very legible. The newspaper may have house names instead of the generic names of Roman or Sanserif. Roman is the style used for the title of this book on the inside cover; it is, as its name implies, a classic style. Its thick and thin strokes with the little serif tails give it an elegant appearance. Sanserif is more robust and, although it has been in existence for many years, it is regarded as modern. The strokes are of equal thickness and, as the name says, there are no serifs at the top and bottom strokes.

These two styles are generally available in three widths, but condensed or expanded are not much used unless they are specially requested or the space for the line is too narrow or too wide. The newspaper will have other typefaces too. When you have chosen the style and width you want, try to use the same type always as part of your identity.

Most types also come in different thicknesses—bold, medium, and light, and maybe extra bold as well. An advertiser will often say 'set bold' thinking that a line may be set in capitals, only to find it is set in heavier type. The popular faces are also available, in certain sizes, in italics.

The art of producing an attractive, readable advertisement consists in not having too many typefaces and sizes.

Preparing your advertisement for the printer

An advertisement has to pass through many hands at the newspaper office—type markers, typesetters, photographers, or even stereotypers (foundrymen) among others. The material needs to be clear and understandable. If the advertisement is not complete artwork, it should be in three parts.

1. *Layout*   A full-size diagram showing where you want the components of the advertisement to be.
2. *Typescript*   All the words that require setting typed out.
3. *Illustrations or artwork*.

The layout should not have all the wording written in. Headline and subheadings should be drawn in position in about the final size that you would like them set. Take care to draw in the capitals and lower case that you require—innumerable capitals turn up in advertisements because the author printed the copy in capitals unthinkingly.

The copy, including the headline, should be typed on separate sheets of paper no larger than A4 and should be double spaced. Each block of copy should be indicated on the layout with straight lines (as in Fig. 7.3) and lettered copy A, B, C. Accurately assessing the size of these blocks of type will come with practice. By consistently using a few standard setting widths you will get to know how many words will fit on a line. If it is not possible to have typewritten copy, clean handwritten copy will do. Typed copy has advantages however: it enables you to keep a carbon copy and is less likely to contain mistakes. Avoid abbreviations, particularly if you are using technical phrases, and don't assume that the reader knows the language of your trade.

Illustrations should be drawn on the layout in the size that you want them to be, but they should be supplied mounted on flat card for preference.

Advertisements presented neatly to the printers encourage the printer to set your advertisement neatly.

Press releases

Most of the big chain stores have a press officer. Some, like Marks and Spencer, have a big department. Small, independent retailers generally do not have a press officer and the only time an independent retailer may feel the need for the services of a press writer is when opening a new branch or extending an existing shop. On these occasions the local newspaper sends someone along to write the necessary article. Its length depends upon the amount of advertising that is being taken by the contractors and suppliers. In these cases there is the distinct danger that everyone, including the retailer, will regard the editorial as mere mortar between the advertising bricks.

A continuous supply of well-written articles, supported with beautiful photography, makes sure chain stores get editorials in the paper with reasonable frequency. If your local newspaper publishes retail press releases and you don't mind withstanding a rejection or two, there is no reason why you shouldn't submit press releases for publication. It's worth a try.

Writing a press release is not difficult provided you remember one or two points. The first essential is to be factual. You should take care also to write in complete sentences and to shun the lavish qualifying adjectives that you may use in an advertisement. A press release is a news story, and should read like one.

The opening paragraph or two should deliver the main gist of the story. An independent store that has dealings with only one newspaper should have the advantage of knowing the type of style of story most likely to be accepted, so it's worth studying your local newspaper features.

The person-to-person approach that is adopted in an advertisement is not suitable for an editorial; the press release has to be written for the impersonal newspaper readership. The third person of an editorial is an advantage to a retailer, especially if it includes quotes from the retailer or, better still, the customers.

New stock arrivals give you the opportunity to issue a press release, new fashions in clothes and furnishings, new kitchen or bathroom equipment, and even the little labour-saving gadgets for the home and garden need just a little creative vision to offer the opportunity to publicize your merchandise.

No editor is likely to publish a story about merchandise or an event that has already appeared in an advertisement. Even to hope to publish the story on the same day as the advertisement prejudices your chances of getting it accepted, especially if there is any similarity between the advertisement and press release or the photographs are the same. Give your release a dateline time for use ahead of the announcement, and send it in advance to allow for scheming on a page that is set up the day before the publication date. This way you avoid competing with the news of the day.

Perhaps the best way to explain the difference between a press release and advertisement copy is to compare an advertisement and an editorial for the opening of an imaginary fashion department in a local store.

A typical advertisement might read:

DISCOVER A NEW WORLD OF FASHION AT FOSTER AND JONES
A new enlarged fashion department opens tomorrow on our first floor. You are invited to our opening continuous fashion shows of the exciting spring ranges from exclusive designers and leading manufacturers. Free coffee.
For one week only we are offering all purchasers a 10 per cent discount.

This would probably be accompanied by an illustration of a dress or coat and selling copy for that garment.

A press release would have a totally different emphasis. A suitable version might be:

New Fashion Floor Opens
Mrs Gillian Foster, wife of Mr Thomas Foster, managing director of Foster and Jones department store, will open a new fashion floor in their extended premises in Cross Street. Mrs Foster, who is the fashion buyer for the store, had very firm ideas about the layout of the new department.

The local architects for the store's structural alterations, Jones and Williams, worked very closely with Mrs Foster who had been on a tour of top fashion houses in Paris for her ideas.

Mrs Foster, who says 'Individual fitting rooms are essential for our type of customer', has had six new fitting rooms built in, each with a full length mirror and curtained in regency style satin. To complete the picture the department is furnished with Louis XIV style armchairs, even in the fitting rooms.

The gilt fittings, mahogany timber and green brocade wallcovering will provide an attractive setting for the continuous fashion show which takes place from 10 a.m. until 4.30 p.m. on Thursday, the opening day.

Mr Thomas Foster, whose father opened the store in 1935, said 'I believe that, despite the economic climate, there is still business to be found for the store that offers quality. When money is scarcer people tend to look for quality even more.'

When you've written your press release, don't be surprised if the newspaper staff reporters rewrite it. Make the release as newsworthy as you can. Include a photograph if possible—for example, one of a dress being worn by a model at the rehearsal.

Rate cards

Booking advertising space in a newspaper is a simple process. Ring your local newspaper and they will generally do the rest. Most will send a representative round to see you.

If you enquire about the cost of advertising, they will supply you with a rate card. Rate cards vary only slightly from one newspaper office to another. Some newspapers issue one rate card for both classified and display advertising and some issue separate rate cards for each. Some rate cards also contain sales matter about the newspaper and the advantages of using it for advertising. The information on the rate card should, of course, be current and for a guide most give the commencement date of the present rate structure.

Apart from the advertising rates and the name(s) of the pulication(s) there is other information that will be of use. The card may contain the circulation figure and state whether the circulation is substantiated by the Audit Bureau of Circulation. If circulation is not on the card then the newspaper may have a separate statement. Most cards have a map showing the area in which the paper circulates. The outer boundary of the circulation area should be governed by the penetration of the newspaper. It generally contains the parishes where at least 10 per cent of the households are taking the newspaper. To determine the most suitable medium it is important to know which newspaper has the best circulation within a four-mile radius of the store, because most people make the majority of their purchases within a four-mile radius of home. Hypermarkets, purpose-built shopping centres and certain specialist retailers are the exceptions to this rule.

The rate card will also contain limited technical data, such as column width and type areas. The column width is quoted for a single column but there are spaces between columns and this has to be accounted for. While one column may be 40 millimetres wide, if there is a 3 millimetre gap between columns a two-column space would be 83 millimetres wide.

Broadsheet newspapers, those that are the size of the quality dailies, *The Times*, the *Daily Telegraph*, etc., have eight, nine or even ten columns to the page. Tabloid newspapers, those that are a similar size to the popular press, have six or seven columns to the page. A more comprehensive rate card will quote the measurements for multi-column widths. Also stated on the card will be the column or page sizes, text pages are from 54 to 63 centimetres and tabloids are 35 to 42 centimetres approximately. These measurements are important if you are going to create advertising that effectively uses every single centimetre of space. It is important to check whether the newspaper requires its artwork or blocks the same size or larger. Some newspapers ask for the larger blocks to allow for shrinkage.

Rate cards will also state what screen is required for halftones (see Chapter 5). If the newspaper quotes screen requirements in greater detail it is best to let your block or bromide maker decipher the instructions.

There is a range of details that may or may not be on the card and they may include:

1. *The type of printing process used*   This is not important in itself but it affects whether the newspaper requires blocks or artwork for reproduction.
2. *'Reverse advertisements not accepted unless with stippled or scored background'*   This rule is inserted on rate cards in the interest of the appearance of the total publication. The newspaper may also reserve the right to stipple or score a solid black background.
3. *Conditions of acceptance*   These have become so extended due to increased government legislation that the rate card may simply say 'Copies of the conditions of acceptance may be had on request.'
4. *ASA levy*   The Advertising Standards Authority is financed by a levy of 0.1 per cent on all display advertising. In the case of

smaller advertisers the levy is paid in bulk by the newspaper.

5. *Spot colour* This is a surcharge for single extra colour in addition to black. The surcharge may be a single sum regardless of size, or a percentage. Most newspapers insist on a minimum size for colour advertisements.

6. *Process colour* Certain web offset newspapers have the facility for using full colour. The surcharge is much higher than for a single colour (see page 136).

7. *Discounts* These are worth asking about, because many newspapers have a range of contract rates for regular advertisers. Most contracts are conditional upon taking an advertisement monthly or weekly, which should be acceptable if you are working to an annual plan. Discount rates may be set out on a separate card.

Deadlines are an essential piece of information carried by rate cards, and they may vary according to the type of advertisement to be submitted. Deadlines for features are often longer than for ROP. Advertisements requiring typesetting or blockmaking often have a longer deadline than complete artwork. Cancellation clauses, if any, can vary according to the advertisement's position in the paper: special positions have a longer deadline and you may incur a financial penalty if you cancel.

Display advertisement rates begin with the standard single-column centimetre rate known as ROP (run of paper) rate and there is usually a minimum depth of three centimetres. Prices of full pages and half pages vary and it is worth checking if these sizes are pro rata to the single column centimetre rate—occasionally some newspapers offer larger spaces at lower rates.

Guaranteed positions are by arrangement and it is normal practice for them to cost more. In practice, on Monday, Tuesday, or Wednesday many papers waive the surcharge because on these days demand is lower.

Remember that position in the newspaper is not the only factor that decides an advertisement's effectiveness. A headline alone is more important than position in making sure that the right prospect reads the advertisement. This is no less true where special positions within the newspaper are concerned. Even the front page of a newspaper cannot transform an incompetent advertisement into a good one. However, special positions are shown on the rate card and charged at a much higher rate, and they are worth the extra if used properly. Newspapers invariably make special positions into set sizes in fixed positions; most have front page positions, many have back page positions, and some have special spots at special prices against the TV guide, on centre pages and the leader page.

Special positions are only worth buying if they fit into your advertising plan and are about the size of space you need on the right day to do the job adequately. In other words, don't reduce the number of words or items to fit a special position or increase your copy to fill a special position, and don't take an advertisement on a different date just to take advantage of a special position.

Title corners—those little announcements adjacent to the newspaper title on the front page—are also shown on the rate card, even if these coveted spots are not available. Don't be dismayed if you can't get one. Console yourself with the reflection that most of them are misused. The only effective way for a retailer to use title corners, sometimes called 'ear pieces', is to put a single hot bargain in each time or advertise one of the store services.

'Financial advertising', another heading to be found on rate cards, refers to prospectuses and company meeting announcements. It is shown separately because some newspapers charge extra for it. It is not normal for a retailer to want this service unless the company is publicly quoted.

Only certain parts of a classified rate card will interest the retailer from a business point of view. However, it is immediately apparent that private advertising is cheaper than trade advertising. The reduced rate for private advertising is to encourage the public to use and read the classified columns. Classified display advertising is more expensive than semi-display and prices can vary between categories. Most quote a series rate for repeating the same advertisement a given number of times.

Radio rate cards

A radio rate card should show the radio reception area and the date on which the rates were fixed, probably on the front page of the card.

The actual rates are shown on a table. Down the left-hand side of the table are the time segments. Audience density varies according to the time of day: prime time in the week is 06.00 to 10.00 hours and it is classified with three As. On Saturday and Sunday triple A time starts and finishes a little later, 08.00 to 14.00 hours. There are four or five time segments AAA, AA, A, B, and C. The smallest audiences are at night. B is the evening, 19.00 hours to close and C is for those stations that broadcast right through the night.

The next column will be the length of the spot, with time lengths from 10 seconds to a minute. In the subsequent columns from left to right are the rates according to the number of spots taken. Taking 50 or more spots in the same time segment can show a saving of up to 15 per cent from the base price of a single spot. The longer the spot, the lower per second the cost is.

Prices vary widely from one segment to another. For example, the cost of prime time is five times greater than that of evening time. Most stations have an audience profile and will supply details upon request to help you evaluate the quantity and quality of their audience. Annual contracts are available and they may be stated on the same card. They offer an extra saving of up to 30 per cent. Annual contracts are agreed with the stations in advance, in writing, for a specified 12-month period.

Package plans are almost sure to be shown on the card. The packages spread the spots evenly over seven days. For example, one package offered by Radio 210 will rotate your spots evenly over the top three time segments. AAA will take 30 per cent of the spots, AA will take 30 per cent and A will take 40 per cent. In this package an advertiser can get 60-second spots for as little as £32 against £57.25 for an equivalent package purely in the AAA segment. On the same card there is a lower-cost plan which includes spots in the B segment. Multi-spot packages are normally rotated from Monday to Sunday on a weekly basis within the segments(s) booked.

Rate cards may also state that extra spots, packages of mixed-length spots, and packages of more than one segment may be purchased pro rata to that rate.

Time segments can change from station to station and from time to time according to the latest audience profile. On Radio 210 rate card the time segments are:

AAA   Mon–Fri 06.00–10.00 hrs;   Sat, Sun 08.00–14.00 hrs
AA   Mon–Fri 10.00–14.00 hrs;   Sat, Sun 06.00–08.00 hrs
A   14.00–19.00 hrs
B   19.00–close

Although the rate card caters only for spots up to 60 seconds in length, longer advertisements are available pro rata. Bookings are accepted for specific days of the week at a surcharge and within a specific half hour for a further surcharge.

It is possible to buy a single advertisement, but with radio it is not desirable. Repetition allows the advertiser to reach more people and registers on subsequent broadcasts. The advantage to buying a package, in addition to its lower cost, is that during the course of a week an advertiser will have reached the widest possible number of listeners, ranging from those who are exclusively morning listeners to those who listen late at night.

Regional Newspaper Advertising Bureau (RNAB)

The major retailing groups in the UK have made a fine art of obtaining advertising funds from their suppliers. Smaller retail outlets have lacked the purchasing muscle to follow suit. However, the Regional Newspaper Advertising Bureau maintains a structured system to enable manufacturers to support their retailers with advertising funds. Any regional newspaper can provide details of available support schemes to any retailer.

Member newspapers of the Bureau were given details in 1981 of 913 national advertisers willing to support retailers with advertising funds. The Bureau also administered 76 advertising campaigns, advising retailers of co-operative schemes by suppliers. Some of these were tied to the retailers' level of purchasing. The Bureau has direct influence over a sales force of 2500 individuals employed by its member newspapers. It is their job to explain details of supplier schemes to retailers and to help retailers in the design of shared advertisements.

While most individual retailers may be well aware of their catchment areas and the media covering that area, the Bureau maintains a computerized data base that links newspaper coverage data with population statistics in approaching 9000 specific areas of the UK.

The Newspaper Society

The Newspaper Society is the 'Trade association' of the regional and local press. Founded in 1836, it now has over 1200 newspapers in membership, and combined circulations are in excess of 8.5 million a day for the dailies and 13 million a week for the weeklies.

The Newspaper Society provides a range of services to help its members with retail advertising. Research and surveys are commissioned on their behalf, and a flow of information and publications supplied for their use. Where necessary, the NS acts with other industry bodies in joint research, campaigns or promotions. Each year, there are competitions for both display and classified advertisements, and the follow-up publications are a source of inspiration and ideas for newspapers and clients alike.

Adformats was pioneered by the NS on behalf of its members with the aim of simplifying the use of the regional press by advertisers who wish to use more than one newspaper. By classifying papers' advertisement sizes into one of five categories (or Adformats), media and production problems are greatly eased for the client and the agency.

The NS training department runs a number of courses, including those for advertisement sales representatives. Such courses include copywriting, advertisement layout, planned advertising, and cooperative advertising. The NS also has its own advertising control department, which offers advice to members on the acceptability of advertisements and provides guidance on the plethora of legislation applicable to them.

Free Newspapers

Good free newspapers offer an unrivalled household penetration. But you need to know whether the quantity and quality of the editorial is sufficient to get itself read, and whether the newspaper is one with which you would wish to be associated.

There can, however, be problems albeit less frequently now, with distributions not being reliable. Intending users should check the paper's distribution system, a good free sheet operator has a back checking system to test their distribution force. It is reassuring if the distribution is a VFD (Verified Free Distribution) figure. VFD is a subsidiary of Audit Bureau of Circulations Ltd.

The system works by a combination of inspection by VFD and audits by independent accountants. Once a newspaper has applied to join the scheme, the publication's records and distribution are scrutinized by a VFD inspector to confirm good record keeping and distribution control. The latter must include agreed standards of back-checking of delivered copies to households on a regular and systematic basis. Further VFD inspections are carried out as a matter of routine.

Success factors

1. *Begin with a few pounds* The smallest retailer can start advertising for a few pounds with classified advertising.
2. *Divide long classified advertisements* When you have a lot of items to list divide them between several individual advertisements.
3. *Use classifieds daily* Classified advertising offers the opportunity of continuity.
4. *Colour for impact* Use spot colour in bold eye-catching masses.
5. *Colour relieves monotony* Spot colour can be used to break up large areas of black type into readable segments.
6. *Test your coupon advertisement* If your local newspaper can do it, test your coupon advertisements with a split run.
7. *Give a reason* Coupons are used more readily if there is a reason given for using them.
8. *Make campaigns interesting* Avoid a boring campaign by making each advertisement in it interesting.
9. *Neat copy inspires printers* Well-presented copy for the printers encourages neat setting.
10. *Send in press releases* Send press releases to your newspaper for new stock arrivals and store developments.
11. *Early and accurate* Give all the facts and send your press releases to your newspaper ahead of the advertisement.
12. *Select the most suitable medium* Most people buy within a radius of four miles of home. Choose the newspaper with the best circulation within four miles of your store.
13. *Special positions can be worth the extra* But don't change the day or size of your intended advertisement just to get a special position in the newspaper.
14. *Reach more listeners with a package* Buy your radio advertising in a package over several time segments if you wish to reach the optimum number of prospects.

14

How far can you go?

It will come as no surprise to the reader of this book to hear that the majority of retailers are not only honest but instinctively fair traders.

Code of Advertising Practice

Although it has frequently been considered by several governments, there is no statutory control on the practice of advertising. There is, however, a voluntary control system which adheres to the British Code of Advertising Practice. Breach of this code is not necessarily an offence against the law, nor does it even give rise to a civil claim.

Most of the regional newspapers of this country, both daily and weekly, belong to the Newspaper Society, which gives guidance to members on how to keep within CAP rules. Newspapers are also interested in protecting their readers. The combination of fair trading retailers and protective newspapers generally means that there are few transgressions.

Advertising Standards Authority

The consumers' watchdog in printed advertising is the Advertising Standards Authority, an organization directly or indirectly financed by the advertisers. Advertising agents pay a modest levy on each advertisement they place and the newspaper pays the levy on directly-placed advertising.

The ASA investigates every complaint sent in by the public, and newspapers frequently donate space to the Authority, which sets out the criteria by asking 'Is it legal? Is it decent? Is it honest?' and giving the address of the Authority for those who wish to complain.

In addition to dealing with complaints, they undertake three types of monitoring. The first is the routine scrutiny of certain publications—the national daily and Sunday newspapers and their supplements, the London evening newspapers, and a selection of regional morning and evening newspapers. The Authority also examines a random selection of regional weekly newspapers, the top-selling weekly and monthly magazines, and a changing selection of 10 to 15 other consumer publications each month.

The Authority's second task is topic monitoring, the checking of advertisements in particular categories that have been the source of public complaint to the ASA or the subject of public concern of topical interest. This type of monitoring is intensive for a short period, generally at seasonal peaks or new product booms. For example, over 500 advertisements for Royal Wedding souvenirs were examined (only 15 of these required investigation, and most of those either failed to explain on what basis 'limited editions' were limited or made unsupported claims about the likely future value of items on offer).

The third type of monitoring is quota monitoring. This follows the principle adopted by the Office of Fair Trading by drawing a sample of advertisements and ascertaining the advertiser's ability effectively to substantiate the claims made by the advertising. There does not have to be an observed contravention to justify this sort of investigation. The principle is to tell the advertiser, 'You have made this claim. Please prove its validity.' A representative selection of publications is scrutinized by the Authority over a four-week period and a balanced coverage by all printed media over the course of a year.

The Authority publishes regular case reports which are sent to editors of all media and can result in adverse publicity for the worst or most persistent offenders. The advertisement departments of newspapers are alerted and, because any reputable publication treasures the goodwill of its readers, they are not likely to publish the offending advertisement again. Persistent offenders are in danger of having all their advertising refused.

In a typical month the Authority received 466 complaints, of which 118 were investigated and 85 had already been investigated. A further 84 had no apparent case to investigate under the terms of the code. The ASA is concerned only with the printed media, and therefore 102 complaints were outside their brief. However, 35 of these were referred to the Independent Broadcasting Authority, the body concerned with commercial radio and television monitoring. The remaining complaints failed to give sufficient details for the ASA to proceed further. Mail order is a big source of complaints. Thirty-eight of the 118 complaints concerned mail-order delays.

Retail complaints

Considering the number of retail outlets and their percentage share of all sales, retail advertisers can feel reasonably proud of their record. However, even this could be improved with a little extra attention in the areas where transgressions occur.

A common fault is ambiguity, generally through carelessness. No doubt the citizens' band radio dealer of London N1 had no intention of misleading the public when the dealer advertised '£5 worth of free CB equipment on this month's CB brochures'. When asking for the brochure, a member of the public was told that the £5 worth of free goods were conditional upon buying £15 worth of goods. The ASA upheld the complaint and the advertiser agreed in future advertisements to include the words 'on orders over £15'. If you follow the advice of an earlier chapter and read the copy out loud to someone else who is listening from the customer's point of view, you should avoid this problem. Not only will you be checking the copy for good sales sense, you will be checking it for omissions and ambiguities.

When it comes to feedback from the sales floor, the smaller retailer has an advantage over the larger one, who may advertise through an agent, on the current stock position. One do-it-yourself operator was advertising a motorized lawn mower throughout April, but by mid-April the entire stock had been sold. The operator had seriously underestimated demand for this particular item. While the ASA did not uphold the complaint, the advertiser did not include the mowers in advertisements after April. It is obvious that no retailer wishes to use valuable advertising space to advertise merchandise that isn't available, achieving ill will in the process. No doubt this sophisticated advertiser was working to some plan (it was a multiple do-it-yourself warehouse chain with an advertising agent), but a small retailer placing advertising direct can work to a plan and use the flexibility the newspaper offers.

One of the golden rules is to monitor the sales of items in each advertisement, and change the items as necessary. In the case above, the feedback from the sales staff in the branch was not getting back fast enough to the advertising department and the advertising agency.

Ambiguity can occur when a retailer also trades by mail order, as in the case of a menswear chain when a member of the public complained that a £10 discount voucher featured in a press advertisement was not honoured on presentation at one of the advertiser's retail branches. He was told that the voucher was valid for orders made from the summer catalogue for outsize garments only, whereas the complainant had ordered standard sizes. The complaint was upheld. The Authority felt there was an element of ambiguity in the wording of the advertisement, which the advertisers explained had been intended to appeal to larger-size customers who could place orders through their mail-order service. The company's catalogue stated that regular sizes of certain garments were obtainable direct at their retail branches and these two statements, taken in conjunction, were potentially misleading for the customer. The company gave an undertaking that future advertising material would be suitably clarified.

Illustrate the right product

A problem for most advertisers is finding an illustration that relates to the copy, and often a picture similar to the advertised product is used. Take the case of a bedding centre with a press advertisement headlined 'Fantastic Price Reductions', illustrated by a three-foot divan set at £36.95. The complainant stated that the illustration did not resemble the bed that was being offered for sale and she further maintained that the bed on offer had been on sale for £36.95 seven months previously.

The first complaint was upheld. The advertisers confirmed that the illustration was not of the bed and had been included in the advertisement in error. They gave their assurance that future copy would be appropriately illustrated. The second complaint was not upheld. The advertisers submitted evidence that satisfied the

Authority that the bed on sale seven months earlier was a different bed and that the advertised reduction on the three-foot divan set was genuine.

Substantiation

Lack of substantiation is another common fault. The claim of an advertiser may be true but that is of little consequence if the statement cannot be proved. Beware if your advertisement makes an extreme claim like 'the highest', or 'the lowest', 'the largest' or even 'the smallest', as in the case where a member of the public objected to a camera dealer's advertisement for camera lenses. The advertisement claimed that the Tamron 500 millimetre f8 SP Tele-Macro CAT lens 'is currently the smallest and lightest lens of that focal length in the world', but the objector believed that smaller and lighter lenses of the same focal length were produced by other manufacturers. Upon investigation it turned out that until recently the Tamron lens in question had been the smallest and lightest lens of that focal length produced, but that the company was aware that new lenses were constantly being manufactured and that the claim was therefore no longer appropriate. They took steps to amend the copy and apologized for the inaccuracy of the claim.

One London jeans retailer made a claim in an advertisement which he could not substantiate—quite a surprising error in view of the fact that this retailer uses an advertising agent and agents are usually more careful in their claims. The statement ran: 'D_____ D_____'s has forced hundreds of shops to do as it does and rely on a small mark-up and fast turnover for profits instead of the usual 100–200% mark up, still very common.' According to the ASA report, the complaint came from a member of the public who doubted that a retail mark-up of 100–200 per cent was very common. The claim was the type of provocative statement that a competitor could equally well have seized upon. Because the advertiser was unable to support the claim with up-to-date statistics relating to the mark-up on retail clothing, the complaint was upheld.

The next substantiation complaint was made against a food store. It was not upheld but drew the comment from the Authority that the basis of the claim should have been stated. A member of the public objected to the claim 'You can't shop cheaper in Chelmsford' in a four-page advertisement for 'The Great New Food Shopping Centre of Chelmsford'. The complainant challenged the claim, and maintained that certain goods were available elsewhere at a cheaper price. The advertisers stated that the claim did not relate to individual items, some of which they accepted could be obtained cheaper elsewhere, but to an overall shopping proposal. This was based on the *Financial Times* shopping basket, which they maintained covered a wide range of items that could typically represent those goods bought on a normal shopping trip. The total price charged by the advertisers for 104 common grocery and household items had been compared with the total price charged by one of their competitors who, the advertisers maintained, had been the cheapest store in the area prior to their opening.

Testimonials make good selling copy and they are even more potent if you can name names and sources, an additional benefit to substantiating sales points.

Prices

There should be no question of ambiguity when it comes to prices quoted in advertisements. The rules are clear where an advertiser uses a price. According to the Code:

> The price should be stated clearly and unambiguously; should be that at which the product is available to the consumer and normally should include the prices of all fixed, non-optional extras.

That seems to be explicit enough but still there are cases of transgressions. Retailers who run lots of price promotions and sales are the most frequent violators of the Code, like the photographic dealer who for one month offered a cash rebate on certain products. A customer challenged the advertised cash rebate price of £33.95 for the 283 light machine on the grounds that he was charged £37.95 for this product at another branch during the month. The Authority upheld the complaint and the advertiser apologized and reimbursed the customer.

The code is equally explicit about reduced prices. It should be clear whether the reduction is reduced from a manufacturer's recommended price, the advertiser's own previous price, the price charged by other retailers, or based on an assessment of the value of the product.

However, some retailers tend to make life complicated, like the large furniture group that published an advertisement headed 'SALE! SAVE! SAVE! SAVE! EVERY SINGLE THING REDUCED!' A complainant pointed out that, according to the body copy, the reductions were made against higher prices to be charged in the future, and he questioned the acceptability of describing current prices as 'reductions'. The advertisers stated that the majority of the items shown in the advertisement were lines regularly stocked by their stores and had been on display prior to the sale commencement date for various periods at the prices quoted in the advertisement as being applicable on 31 August. The formula 'by 31 August' had been used in order not to conflict with the Trade Description Act 1968 and Price Marking (Bargain Offers) Orders 1979, since the advertisers were not in a position to assert categorically that all items advertised had been in stock, in all stores, for the requisite number of days or had been previously sold in specific stores at the higher prices quoted. Although the Authority considered that, read as a whole, the advertisement was not likely to mislead, they thought it unfortunate that, in these circumstances, the word 'reduced' had been chosen to encapsulate the offer.

As the Code itself points out, the Code's rules are not the only ones to affect advertising. There are many provisions, both in the common law and in statutes, that can determine the form or content of an advertisement. The Code is not in competition with the law. Its rules and the machinery through which they are enforced are designed to complement legal controls, not to usurp or replace them.

Plainly the Code has one advantage over the law and that is the spirit of its enforcement. Once any guidelines are made into laws the charlatan can find a way of exploiting their wording to his advantage. As the Code stands, advertisers, agents, and media have a clear idea of the intention, and its control takes place at all of these levels. There are over 70 common law rights that can also impinge on advertising and approximately 25 of them relate to retail practices. If any complaint involves legal rules, professional advice should be sought when in doubt. The key laws that are most frequently broken are those relating to hire purchase, fair trading, food and drugs, mail-order transactions, prices, and trade descriptions.

'Honesty is the best policy' is an adage that is made more apt by the focus that advertising gives it. Every single advertisement is a little bit of your store and your policy pushed into the glare of the limelight as it reaches more homes than the mind can comprehend. It must be worth the time and trouble to get things right, not just to avoid friction with customers but to make more sales and create goodwill. It must equally repay the retailer in sales and goodwill to give staff clear guidelines on how to achieve speedy settlement of complaints.

The rules and radio

Advertising on radio and television is governed by the IBA Code of Advertising Standards and Practice. It is a comprehensive document of general rules and three main appendices which deal in detail with advertising in relation to children, financial advertising, and the advertising of medicines and treatment. The rules are not dissimilar from those of the ASA but there are some differences. For example, a lot of attention is paid to presentation, particularly if it offends religious sects or physically disabled people, or is unsuitable for children to listen to.

Advertising has to be vetted before being broadcast and this, combined with the fact that there are far fewer advertisements, means that radio advertising is the subject of far fewer complaints than advertising in the press. During 1980–81 over 850 letters and telephone calls or comments were received from viewers and listeners. The great majority related to minor matters; some related to the difficulties experienced in obtaining advertised products. Only nine complaints were upheld—five relating to television advertising and four relating to independent local radio advertising, one of which might be regarded as retail advertising (the case of a business machine advertisement quoting prices that did not include VAT). One of the TV complaints was similar to cases of transgressions in the press, namely a case of Sunday trading in breach of the Shops Act.

The IBA's concern over the presentation of advertising was illustrated on one occasion by a commercial shown before Christmas, in which a well-known comedian was seen 'stealing' goods for a stage display. Retailers were among many who complained that this was condoning shop-lifting at a time of year when store pilfering was at its peak. This shows the other side to the 'theatre of the mind' that broadcasting achieves.

Any retailer who intends to use either radio or television to advertise should get a copy of the IBA Code.

The IBA Code of Advertising Standards and Practice

Broadcasting, because of its intimacy within the home gives rise to problems that do not occur in the press. As the IBA Code states, broadcast advertising should be legal, decent, and honest, so advertisements have to comply with the same common laws or statutes for radio as for newspapers. Another similarity is that broadcast advertisements must be recognizably separate from programme material, just as press advertisements must be distinguishable from editorials. For example, the introduction to a broadcast advertisement must not use the words 'news flash'.

Item number 14 of the Code reads, rather vaguely: 'Audible matter in advertisements must not be excessively noisy or strident.' This rule exists to give the station the right to cut out any noise that may alarm. Keeping to this rule should not present a problem because all good advertising should whisper seductively rather than shout.

To sum up, a retailer should adopt the same legal and honest principles in radio advertising as in newspaper advertising. Broadcasting puts a new slant on what might be regarded as decent, but presumably your advertisement will be made by either the radio station or a professional recording studio that knows the rules.

A speedy clearance of local radio advertisements is achieved by the radio company staff, who are experienced in the field of copy control and in consultation with IBA staff.

Newspaper publishers and radio stations may impose stricter standards than those laid down by either the ASA or the IBA.

Success factors

1. *Be unambiguous*   Careless copywriting causes complaints and creates ill will.

2. *Read your copy out loud*   By reading your copy out loud, prefer-ably to someone else listening from the reader's point of view, you will eliminate misleading, goodwill-killing statements.

3. *Monitor your response and your stocks*   After every advertisement check your sales of advertised lines and remaining stocks before re-advertising the same lines.

4. *Word coupons carefully*   State what items they are redeemable against and put in an offer ending date, if there is one.

5. *Use the correct illustration*   Make sure the picture of the product relates to the description and price in the copy.

6. *Substantiate your claims*   Only say 'largest', 'cheapest', or even 'best' if you can prove it. Better still, put the substantiation in the advertisement.

7. *Seek professional help*   If a complaint involves common law and you are in doubt, get professional help.

8. *Maintain good communications*   A well-briefed staff will stop com-plaints escalating.

9. *Know the rules*   Get copies of both the ASA and IBA Codes of Advertising practice.

The rules of advertising increase the public's trust in advertising

15.

What happens when I grow bigger?

There can be no doubt that the retailer who advertises correctly will prosper, not only because advertising improves sales but because it also puts the entire retail operation under pressure. It's like pressing the accelerator of a motor car, but instead it is a profit machine.

Advertising sets the pace for every function of the store. If you are selling faster you have to buy faster. If the store traffic increases, the floor space has to accommodate the extra people, and every square foot begins to matter more. If there are more customers, the sales staff have to be more expeditious. If the stock turns over faster, the cash flow improves. If the cash flow improves, interest payments are lower and the need for credit decreases. If goods move faster and credit time decreases, your influence over suppliers increases. In every way the business is going better.

Three phases of business

It's not long, therefore, before the successful retailer is looking for more floor space and more staff to continue expanding. It is difficult to stand still—a business must generate or degenerate. Retailers who believe that it is possible to open a business and stay still should beware, for all businesses, after a period of struggling upwards from the start, reach the plateau of security. This period when sales are going well and the outgoings are contained can, unfortunately, also be a period of complacency.

The largest of multiple retailers have encountered this complacency period and its time span can vary. The uphill climb can be a long one, taking as much as 10 years. The period of complacency can be even longer. What inevitably follows it is a period of degeneration.

There are symptoms that distinguish complacency from the agonism of the secure business; lack of communication through the key controllers of the business to the staff, no training, indifferent stock control, no sales goals, and the belief that selling in advertising is not necessary.

Advertising in the complacent period tends to be egotistical rather than sales orientated. Even to the very end there are retailers who take an ego trip with each advertisement. I remember one closing-down advertisement headlined 'Mr. M– is retiring after 30 years of public service to this town and is offering his best ever bargain in his CLOSING DOWN SALE'. This was the last advertisement in 10 years of self-indulgent advertising, in which he put his picture in each advertisement and began to philosophize rather than merchandise.

The secret of success is to keep to the golden rules. The principles of professional selling in print were researched and tested in the 'thirties. Clyde Bedell first published these principles in 1940 in his book *How to Write Advertising that Sells*. Although the book was subsequently updated, the principles didn't change. Those principles are used in this book in chapters that deal with copy and headlines. No matter how big your business grows, keep to these golden rules and your growth will continue.

Keeping to the success formulae may be difficult because the more branches a business has, the more likely there is to be a breakdown in communications, as in the case of the do-it-yourself warehouse in Chapter 14 which advertised lawn mowers while they were out of stock. The more department heads there are, the greater the likelihood there is of having some buyers with a lower enthusiasm or ability to find promotable stock.

No matter how big a retail business may be, the first success factor has got to be having the right merchandise in sufficient quantities to make the advertisement effective. Merchandise is the magnet that draws the crowds and establishes your reputation. The inability of a store to meet its advertised promises is not only wasteful but a source of disesteem. Never repeat an advertisement without knowing that there is sufficient of the advertised stock available at each branch. An unbroken, reliable chain of communication from the points of sale to the advertising controller is essential.

When you need an advertising agent

A retailer could handle up to approximately 7000 column centimetres of newspaper advertising a year successfully himself with the aid of newspaper advertising staff. There are those who place more advertising than this, but their total generally includes a lot of repeats and advertising that does not have sales energy. To be effective with an advertising budget that uses more than 7000 column centimetres, help is needed—yet if your expenditure is below £100 000 it is unlikely that a good agency would be interested in the account.

Any growing retailer must go through a period when advertising requires a conscious effort by all department managers to write copy and find illustrations to fulfil their role in the advertising plan.

A suitable freelance artist can be found for whatever finished artwork is necessary, and one advantage of a consistent advertising style is that it becomes a system easily understood by everybody involved in production: the store staff who write the copy, the person who lays out the advertisement, and the newspaper staff who do the typesetting.

However, eventually you will have no alternative but to pass your advertising to an agent, who will get part of his income from the newspaper. The majority of newspapers pay 15 per cent commission to the agency. But an agency cannot exist on the 15 per cent paid by newspapers alone and will almost certainly make a service charge, in addition to any block or artwork charges.

It is essential to keep these ancillary costs down to a minimum to enable the largest portion of the budget to go into maximum coverage with the largest possible advertisements. However, many an agent's charges could be funded out of the space that is now being wasted by advertisers who are placing their advertising direct with the newspaper.

Advertisements prepared by agents are generally better than those produced by the average retailer, but really this is due more to a lack of professionalism by the retailer than to the professionalism of the agency.

Type of agent

A retailer choosing an agency should look out for one with retail experience. A large number of national agencies tend to specialize in manufacturers' consumer advertising, where their creative talents are not hampered by a shortage of funds.

For product advertising, the economy of scale is very much in favour of a highly professional, slick type of advertising. However, if mistakes are made they are big ones. Media production costs for each advertisement, although high, are probably lower per prospect reached, because national media are being used. Similarly, the administration costs are lower because fewer invoices and less checking are necessary.

The shrewd retailer will be uneasy about the system, prevalent in the agency business, of taking commission on production expenditure. For large agencies who book large television campaigns, commission from production studios forms an important source of net profit. Even smaller agents get commission from typesetting houses and art studios.

This amounts to a costs-plus-profit system and removes any incentive to control costs.

You may feel that the entire commission system, even for space bookings, is not conducive to furthering the advertiser's best interests. Image campaigns without specific merchandise, repeat advertising, fewer but larger advertisements and more expensive media offer greater net profit for the irresponsible agent.

The top retailers use national media, mostly newspapers; a smaller number use television, because they have enough outlets to match the coverage and keep wasted circulation to a minimum, or even eliminate it altogether if they have branches within reach of everyone. Centralized advertisement bookings need a centralized merchandising system if an 'out of stock' situation is to be avoided.

Many provincial agents specialize in trade and technical advertising. Their experience lies in placing 'situations vacant' advertising and trade advertising in the specialist press. Their communication expertise is in the 'business to business' sphere. There is, however, a growing number of agents who see the potential in retail advertising. These agents know the problems, have good ideas and are capable of eliminating waste.

To find the right agency you need to invite several to present to you reasons why you should choose them. The advertisement manager of your local newspaper should be able to advise you on a suitable agent. If you see a style of advertising that you think would meet your needs ask which agent handles that account.

Finding an agent

If the advertisement manager cannot help or is unable to provide you with sufficient names, he will probably be able to show you a copy of the BRAD (British Rate and Data) advertising agency list, which will give you more names from which to choose. *Campaign*, the magazine of the advertising business, also publishes a portfolio containing the names, addresses and examples of British advertising agents. The majority of reputable agents belong to the IPA (Incorporated Practitioners in Advertising) and they too have a list of members and guidelines for choosing an agency.

The next stage is to ask your chosen candidates if they are interested in taking on your account. If they are, invite them along to tell you why, and even how, they will do a good job for you. Some agencies charge for this initial presentation and, in view of the importance of procuring the services of the right agency, this charge is of little consequence.

From you the successful agency will expect an accurate assessment of your objectives, including your sales and profit plan. You expect the agency to have a clear idea of your image and position in the marketplace. You also expect the agency to have a creative aptitude that will reflect the character of your business and, at the same time, sell merchandise. Beware of agents who try to sell the idea that the most effective advertising sells the store alone—this is the easy route that bypasses the problems associated with merchandise advertising. Whatever agency you choose should have the resources to produce an advertisement in the limited time between your supplying the details of the merchandise and the newspaper deadline.

Communications

Your agent will need from you a clear brief and your cooperation with the production of each advertisement. Clarity is important and it would be better for all if the details were set down on paper so that everyone, both in the agency and your store, who contributed to the sales plan knew the objectives, the strategy, and their role in the plan. Time to an advertising agency is money, and profitability is governed by the most effective use of that time. You will in effect be paying for your agency's time by the hour, so don't waste it through lack of direction.

Having an agent is like having a part-time member of the staff, and it is desirable to treat the agency like a member of the staff. The entire agency is part of your creative alliance. The copywriter should work closely with the buyers, because no one should write copy for merchandise they haven't seen. The creative head should visit the store regularly to ensure that the agency has a clear image of the store. One of the disadvantages of having an agent is that the advertising may not be consistent with the store image.

Robert Townsend, chairman of Avis Rent A Car, asked this question of each presenting agency: 'How do you get five million dollars of advertising for one million dollars?' Bill Bernbach, of advertising agents Doyle, Dane, Bernbach, came up with the right answer. He asked for 90 days to learn enough about the business to devise an advertising strategy. Bernbach came to the simple conclusion that Avis wasn't the largest car rental firm and that the employees were trying harder. The rest is history. DDB produced a headline that became famous and was emulated by many others.

The account executive who handles your account will need the details of your advertising plan and, in subsequent years, should be instrumental in its initiation. A degree of confidence in the account executive is necessary because, ideally, he or she needs to know the sales goal and the actual achievement to be of real help. The account executive needs to know how you arrived at your sales goal, what percentage of it you are prepared to spend on advertising, and how much of the advertising budget, in addition to the contingency fund, you are prepared to allocate to production and handling costs.

Having an agent does not mean relaxing your determination to ensure that every department gets an advertising allocation every month to help achieve its sales goal. For the retailer who may have expanded into several branches in other towns, the agent can help extend the principle to each branch by making sure that each one gets adequate advertising support in the right newspaper.

Keeping a set of standards is important, with or without an agent. A set of questions can form the basis of your guidelines for each advertisement.

Keep a check on your advertising

The preceding chapters have formed the basis for the questions you should ask of each advertisement before insertion. It is easier to lapse in your standards when you have delegated the responsibilty for your advertising, so this 47-question checklist should be used. The answer to the first three questions must be yes or there is no point in publishing the advertisement.

1. Is the merchandise of a quality that we are proud to offer our type of customer?
2. Is the merchandise sellable at this time of the year?
3. Do we have sufficient quantity to make the advertisement worth while?
4. Does the advertisement have smaller allied items to make each potential transaction larger and maximize store traffic?
5. Does the advertisement address the prospect at whom it is aimed?
6. Does the headline promise the prospect a benefit?
7. Will the prospect want to read on after reading the headline?
8. Does the advertisement sell to the maximum number of prospects?
9. Does the advertisement reflect the store's expertise?
10. Is news used in the headline?
11. Are subheads used to break up long copy or head up each departmental section?
12. Does each subhead promise a benefit?
13. Does the body copy use selling points and promise benefits?
14. Are prices used?
15. Are prices offset by corresponding benefits? Is it the case that the greater the price, the more and better the benefits?
16. Does the copy anticipate objections and effectively answer them?
17. Does the advertisement carry conviction?
18. Have sufficient questions been answered for the maximum number of prospects to come and see the merchandise?

19. Is there a sense of urgency about the offer?
20. Does the advertisement have an illustration?
21. Is the illustration relevant?
22. Does the illustration show the product in use and to the product's best advantage?
23. Is the item described the same item that is illustrated?
24. Is the main illustration used dominantly and imaginatively?
25. Does the advertisement use the store's full name and address?
26. Does the advertisement contain extra information, like telephone number, car parking facilities, hours of business, credit facilities, when established, etc.?
27. Are the name, address, and other details contained within a proportionate amount of space?
28. Does the advertisement reflect the store image?
29. Is it consistent with past advertising, your displays, and your showcards?
30. Is every centimetre being used effectively?
31. Is the typesetting tidy?
32. Does the size and the shape of the advertisement reflect the character and size of the store?
33. Are the usual border, slogan, symbol, and logotype being used?
34. Does this advertisement use manufacturers' support?
35. If so, do the first three questions of this checklist apply to the co-operative elements of the advertisement?
36. Will the goods featured in the advertisement be on display in the store?
37. Do the sales people know what items are in this advertisement?
38. Have arrangements been made to ensure the return of manufacturers' contributions?
39. If this advertisement is a repeat, did it do well last time?
40. Is this advertisement different from other retailers but within the unique character of the store?
41. Is the advertisement easy to read? Is the type large enough? Black on white? Body matter not more than two columns wide?
42. Is the proposition clear?
43. Is the layout simple?
44. If it's a big advertisement, is your name at the top and in the middle as well as at the bottom?

45. Is the advertisement legal? Is the copy clear and unambiguous?
46. Is the advertisement decent? Can it be read by all members of the family?
47. Is the advertisement honest? Can you substantiate all the claims you make for the merchandise?

If the answer to all of these is yes, which is unlikely, there will be no problems, only marvellous results. Have the checklist typed out and duplicated and keep a score on each advertisement. The number of yes answers should rise with each advertisement.

After each advertisement a short procedure is also necessary. The first requirement is a guardbook, a scrapbook big enough to accommodate the largest advertisement you are likely to take, together with a few details like where and when the advertisement appeared, and the results the following day and the following week for the items advertised, for the department and for the entire store. Make a note also of the weather if it is extreme or unexpectedly unfavourable to the sale of the featured items. Make a note too of the ancillary charges and record the location of the artwork. Few newspapers retain artwork or blocks after three months, so if you are likely to want to use it again outside that limit, ask for its return. Artwork commissioned and paid for by the advertiser is the advertiser's property and copyright. Other information to be recorded should be cost of the advertisement, date invoice received, date paid, date co-op funds claimed, date received and any relevant comments that may be helpful in considering a repeat at a future date.

Cost control

The aim behind using an advertising agency is to save part of the extra costs by eliminating waste through economic media selection and the most prudent use of space. A conflict occurs when the desire to economize conflicts with the best intentions of an aggressive plan. Savings, after all, are something that a retailer can be sure will make a direct contribution to profit. Despite this, it is preferable to follow the original intention of a merchandise-led advertising plan that regularly changes the offers.

Do not be tempted to use repeats unless they are proven winners, and do not lapse into 'image only' advertising under the mistaken impression that it is only necessary to sell the store.

Legitimate institutional advertising could be used when an unduly large amount of peak-night bargain advertising has tarnished an otherwise quality image. Such advertising, which does not have dated copy, could be used on off-peak days and some daily newspapers will give a substantial discount for advertising with an option of the week insertion clause.

The biggest single production expense can be the cost of artwork or illustrations. The agency may need you to help them by asking your suppliers, well in advance, for photographs or art pulls. The more branches and the more newspapers used, the better the value from the initial production costs if the same merchandise is available at all branches.

The principles applicable to procuring cooperative advertising from manufacturers are just as important with an agency as without. The store's buyers should ask for the manufacturer's financial assistance when they are buying and for special promotions the agency could design visuals to support their proposals.

Apart from the individual checklist for each advertisement, you will naturally want to appraise the plan monthly, actual sales against sales goal, expenditure against budget, cost of artwork and administration charges against budget, departmental performances and the achievement of objectives. The appraisal should be made both for that particular month and cumulatively.

Enthusiasm is the hardest but most desirable attribute for the small retailer to retain as the business expands, especially when you want the right attitudes to spread beyond your own organization to your advertising agent. Every manager, every buyer and, especially, your advertising agency, have got to be in on the act, full participating members of your creative alliance.

Success factors

1. *Beware of complacency* After the initial uphill struggle, businesses reach the plateau of success. It's the danger time for complacency.
2. *Keep to the golden rules* The same rules of good advertising apply even to the biggest retailers.

3. *Make sure advertised goods are available in all branches* Good communications are essential.

4. *Select the right agent* Pick one with retail experience.

5. *Time is money* Your agent's time costs money. Good organization saves the agent's time and your money.

6. *Let the agency get acquainted with your store* The agency staff should be familiar with your store and your objectives.

7. *Copywriters must see the product* The agency copywriters will write better if they see what they have to sell.

8. *Agree a budget* Give every facility to the agency for working out an advertising plan.

9. *Check every advertisement* Use the 48-point checklist to vet every advertisement before it is sent to the newspaper.

10. *Contact suppliers* Even though you have an agent, keep buyers aware of the need to continue getting suppliers' support in the form of advertising funds and illustrations.

Useful reading

Bedell, Clyde (1952) *How to Write Advertising that Sells*, 2nd edn, McGraw-Hill, New York.

Buckley, Earle A. (1961) *How to Increase Sales with Letters*, McGraw-Hill, New York.

Caples, John (1961) *Tested Advertising Methods*, Harper and Row, London.

Foster, Ann and Bill Thomas (1981) *The Retail Handbook*, McGraw-Hill, London.

Ogilvy, David M. (1966) *Confessions of an Advertising Man*, Mayflower-Dell.

Retail Ad. Week Retail Reporting Bureau, New York. UK agent Action Services Advertising, 14 Atherstone Drive, Guisborough, TS14 7BN. A weekly publication with examples of store advertising from America, Canada, and occasionally Australia.

Seklemian, M. (1979) *Sek Says*, Retail Reporting Bureau, New York.

Tack, Alfred (1972) *Profitable Letter Writing*, World's Work Ltd., London.

Glossary

ABC   See Audit Bureau of Circulations.

Advertisement schedule   The programme of advertisements, bookings showing dates, sizes, media, and possibly departments or lines to be featured.

Advertising Standards Authority (ASA)   An organization financed by advertisers which is the consumer's watchdog.

Advertising agents   A company able to book and prepare advertising for advertisers (see also IPA).

Advertising budget   An allocation of funds, usually a percentage of anticipated sales, set aside for the purpose of advertising.

Attention compellor   An advertisement illustration that does not illustrate the product for sale, put in to attract attention.

Audience profile   The type (e.g., age, sex) and number of people who are listening throughout the day.

Audit Bureau of Circulation (ABC)   The letters ABC are often found on rate cards and circulation statements for newspapers and periodicals. They mean that the Bureau verifies that it is an audited average net sale or certificated distribution.

BRAD   See British Rate and Data.

Brand base   A pre-recorded radio advertisement for branded goods onto which a stockist's name and address can be superimposed by the radio station.

British Rate and Data (BRAD)   A monthly publication that lists all the media in the country, (Press, TV, radio and posters) together with current advertising rates. BRAD also publishes a list of advertising agencies.

Broadsheet newspaper   Large-paged newspaper similar to *The Times*.

Campaign A series of advertisements with a recurring theme: also the name of a trade publication for advertising people.

CAP See Code of Advertising Practice.

Cash off the page A term used in mail-order advertising to describe sales directly from an advertisement.

Code of Advertising Practice (CAP) A voluntary control system for printed advertisements, the rules of which are printed in a booklet published by the Advertising Standards Authority.

Contingency budget A percentage of the advertising budget set aside for unexpected events and special entrepreneurial purchases.

Copy The words of the advertisement that are to be placed in the printer's hands, from which the advertisement will be set.

Creative alliance Everyone likely to affect the success of a sales plan working in unison.

Ear piece See Title corner.

Grey cut line A process for converting photographs into crisp-line image for reproduction.

Guardbook A scrapbook for saving cuttings of advertisements and a check on results, cooperative funds, and payment.

Gutter The space between pages down the fold of the newspaper.

Halftone The technical term for photographs that are printed in newspapers, magazines, and other printed material.

Hot metal Jargon for a letterpress printing system (see Letterpress).

IBA See Independent Broadcasting Authority.

Illustration service A syndicated service to which a newspaper subscribes for the franchise to use the artwork within its circulation area. Usually offered to advertisers free of charge.

Incorporated Practitioners in Advertising (IPA) Professional organization for advertising agents.

Independent Broadcasting Authority (IBA) The public board that controls all forms of commercial broadcasting in Britain. It is the country's official instrument of consumer protection on radio and TV advertising. The IBA publish their own Code of Advertising Standards and Practice.

IPA   See incorporated Practitioners in Advertising.

Letterpress   A method of printing newspapers from semi-cylindrical plates cast from lead base metal. Illustrations need to be supplied in the form of matrices, zinc blocks or stereos.

Linear   A fast, cheap conversion process for illustrating advertisements, suitable for retailers.

Logotypes   A signature block cut from your store name or the brand names of manufacturers. A term originally applied to letterpress, still used for web offset processes.

Mezzotint   A photographic process for converting halftones into an irregular screen for printing.

Monitoring   Keeping a record of advertisements that have been published or broadcast and a record of sales following their publication.

Omnibus advertisement   An advertisement that serves more than one department.

Overline   A word or two, often in the form of artwork, that is placed at the top of an advertisement, but not a headline. Often used in campaigns for a special promotion.

Planned advertising   A programme of advertising over a given period to achieve desired results for a controlled expenditure.

Point   Measurement system for type sizes.

Position in the marketplace   The unique segment from which a business draws its custom. The segment can be defined by all or some of the following dimensions: demographics, socio–economic group, hobbies, sports, etc.

Presenter effect   The aura a particular medium has, from which the advertiser benefits if it is favourable.

Process colour   A method of full-colour printing.

Prospects   Potential buyers likely to respond to an advertisement.

Rate of stockturn (RST)   The average rate at which stocks are sold, calculated by this formula:

$$RST = \frac{\text{Total annual sales}}{\text{Average stock}} \text{ (both at selling price)}$$

Regional Newspaper Advertising Bureau (RNAB)   A bureau established by the majority of the regional newspapers to promote advertising in the regional press.

Reverse   Typesetting that has been reversed from black onto white to white on black.

RNAB   See Regional Newspaper Advertising Bureau.

ROP   Run-of-paper advertising placed anywhere on the newspages.

Sales goal   An anticipated value of sales of a given period in a promotional programme.

Sales pattern   A graph showing each month's sales for a particular store, type of store, or product, as a percentage of the year's total.

Scrapertone   A semi-photographic process using fine line to convert photographs into printable image.

Selling point   A feature of the product or service that is necessary if it is to fulfil its function.

Semi-display   A simple style of advertising in the classified columns.

Serif   The tail at the end of the unconnected strokes of a letter in Roman or Roman-type letters ('sanserif' means without a serif).

Socio–economic profile   A marketing expression for a scale that measures family status by social and economic factors.

Subheading   Literally a subsidiary headline. Used for sections of the advertisement on blocks of copy. Subheads indicate the theme of the copy that follows.

Synergism   The effect of recalling the longer version of a broadcast advertisement when a short one is being played, or of seeing the TV picture when only the soundtrack is being broadcast on radio.

Tabloid   Smaller sized newspaper approximately half the size of a text page.

Time segments Radio term for bands of time within the day, which govern the average number of listeners. Each segment is valued accordingly.

Title corner The small advertisements that appear alongside the name of a newspaper on the front page (in some cases on the back page also).

Typeface The style or character of the letters.

Type mark-up This specifies on a visual of an advertisement the size and typeface of the types to be used.

Web offset A method of lithographic printing by newspaper presses. Illustrations supplied to a web offset printer should be artwork, repro proofs, or photographs.

Index